IDEA TO IMAGE
in Photoshop CS2

RICK SAMMON'S
Guide to Enhancing Your Digital Photographs

Rick Sammon

Peachpit Press

Idea to Image in Photoshop CS2
Rick Sammon's Guide to Enhancing Your Digital Photographs

Rick Sammon

Peachpit Press
1249 Eighth Street
Berkeley, CA 94710
510/524-2178
800/293-9444
510/524-2221 (fax)

Find us on the Web at www.peachpit.com
To report errors, please send a note to errata@peachpit.com

Peachpit Press is a division of Pearson Education

Acquisitions Editor: Pam Pfiffner
Editors: Rebecca Gulick, Ted Waitt
Production Editor: Hilal Sala
Image Editor: Mimi Vitetta
Copyeditor: Tiffany Taylor
Proofreader: Liz Welch
Art Director: Charlene Will
Interior Designer and Compositor: Kim Scott, Bumpy Design
Cover Designer: Aren Howell
Indexer: FireCrystal Communications

ISBN 0-321-42918-4
987654321
Printed and bound in the United States of America

Idea to Image is dedicated to Dr. John E. Sarno,
whose books enabled me to travel the world
in search of photographs for this book.

Contents

Acknowledgments

In September 2005, I was at Photoshop World, in Boston, chatting with Pam Pfiffner, Senior Acquisitions Editor at Peachpit Press. During a break in my sessions, we were discussing a possible book. "What kind of book do you *want* to do?" Pam asked me. "We want you to produce a book of which you'd be proud."

I had already been thinking about writing a Photoshop book entitled *Awaken the Artist Within*, which would feature my favorite Photoshop enhancements—as well as my tried-and-true photography techniques. I pitched the idea to Pam. "Let's do it," said PP from PP, as she's known among friends.

Now, less than a year since we shook hands on the idea in Bean Town, the book is going to press. How cool is that!

So, Pam is the first person to whom I'll say "thank you" for all her help, support, encouragement, patience, and nurturing over the past few hectic months of production—all electronic, no less. I also want to thank Pam for coming up with a more appropriate title: *Idea to Image*.

Pam is not the only person at Peachpit Press whom I'd like to thank. Several other folks became part of my life, and, among other things, got to know what a bad proofreader I am (even after 27 books). Here's the impressive list of dedicated behind-the-scenes team members who helped make me look good:

Hilal Sala, Production Editor
Tiffany Taylor, Copyeditor
Liz Welch, Proofreader
Charlene Will, Art Director
Aren Howell, Cover Designer
Kim Scott, Interior Designer and Compositor
Mimi Vitetta, Image Editor
FireCrystal Communications, Indexer
Ted Waitt, Project and Development Editor

But wait! There's one more person at Peachpit Press to whom I owe a big "thank you": Rebecca Gulick, Project and Development Editor. Rebecca was my main editor, molding my copy, images, screenshots, and photographs into chapters and lessons that made this book easy to read and accurate (because she went through all the lessons to make sure I didn't leave out a step). Toward the end of the project, Rebecca took maternity leave. Ted Waitt took over for the mom-to-be, putting the icing on the cake, so to speak.

Enough about Peachpit Press...until my next book with them.

My wife, Susan, and my dad, Robert M. Sammon, Sr., also helped me with the text for this book, reading every lesson and making suggestions that greatly improved the work.

Julieanne Kost, Adobe Evangelist, gets a big "thank you" for inspiring me to get into Photoshop in 1999.

Addy Roff and Victoria Vestal at Adobe also get a big "thank you." Addy has given me the opportunity to share my Photoshop techniques at trade shows around the country.

Other friends in the digital-imaging industry who have helped in one way or another include David Leveen of MacSimply and Rickspixelmagic; Mike Wong and Craig Keudell of onOne Software; Rob Sheppard and Wes Pitts of *Outdoor Photographer* and *PCPhoto* magazines; Ed Sanchez and Mike Slater of Nik Software; George Schaub, editorial director of *Shutterbug* magazine; Scott Kelby and Chris Main of *Layers* magazine; and Bill Lindsay of WACOM.

At Mpix.com, my online digital-imaging lab, I'd like to thank Joe Dellesaga, John Rank, Dick Coleman, and Richard Miller.

Kelly Block, Rick Booth, Dave Metz, Steve Inglima, Peter Tvarkunas, Chuck Westfall, and Rudy Winston of Canon USA have been ardent supporters of my work as well as my photography seminars. My hat is off to these friends, big time! The Canon digital SLRs, lenses, and accessories that I use helped me capture the finest possible pictures for this book.

My photo-workshop students were, and always are, a tremendous inspiration for me. Many have shown me new digital darkroom techniques, some of which I use in this book. During my workshops, I found an old Zen saying to be true: "The teacher learns from the student."

Thank you, one and all. I could not have done it without you!

Introduction

Start Dreaming!

Idea to Image is about how Adobe Photoshop CS2, the most powerful image-editing program for photographers, can help you through the process of turning your ideas into more creative and artistic images—or images that can bring a smile to your face. At a deeper level, this book is about using your imagination—about dreaming in Photoshop to create your own artistic pictures, unique images that no person on the planet has even dreamed (or conjured up).

What will you learn in this book? Plenty, I hope—about Photoshop, photography, and your own creative talent. You'll also learn a bit about me because any book is a reflection (permanent, no less) of the author's personality.

In addition to my favorite Photoshop artistic techniques, illustrated with some of my favorite photographs from around the world, I've included two chapters on photography. "The Photographic Idea" leads off the book, and "The Photographic Image" closes it. (Get it? *Idea to Image*.) These are important chapters, because you must strive to get the best possible and most creative in-camera image. Always.

Sandwiched between the "Idea" and "Image" chapters are the chapters that form the heart of this book: "Image-Enhancement Artistry," "Creative-Image Artistry," and "Advanced-Image Artistry." They offer ideas for cooking up artistic images from your straight shots.

The chapters are lessons that are carefully designed to enhance your learning experience. You can look at them like a menu: "Image-Enhancement Artistry" is the Photoshop appetizer, "Creative-Image Artistry" is the Photoshop main course, and "Advanced Image-Artistry" is the Photoshop dessert.

For each lesson in the middle section, I've included a work image—the photograph that leads off the lesson. You can download these images from the Images page at www.ricksammon.com. Play around with these to your heart's content. Make a screensaver if you like. But please remember that

I hold the copyright on these images, and they are for your own personal use only.

Here are four suggestions about how to approach this book:

1. Read the chapters and lessons in order. You'll learn important techniques in early lessons that you can use in later lessons.

2. Learn one technique at a time, and then practice that technique on your images. Using a music analogy (I attended Berklee College of Music), if you try to master in one week a jazz tune that changes keys five or six times and requires a bunch of thirteenth and minor ninth chords, you'll probably become frustrated, just as I would. But if you try to learn only a few measures and chords per day, or per week, you'll see your progress and be more satisfied with your efforts.

3. When you're applying different effects suggested in this book, play and have fun. Don't take this stuff too seriously. The goal is to create something new and exciting and different—an image that will make you smile. Again, using the music analogy, improvise!

4. Don't be so quick to move on to the next lesson. Experiment with the pull-down menus. Click fly-out arrows here and there. See what other creative possibilities await you.

But what about me, the guy who put all these lessons together for you? To begin, many people say that I'm lucky to have this dream job—travel photographer and writer, author, television host, workshop leader, magazine columnist, and Photoshop instructor. When I hear that, I always respond, "The harder I work, the luckier I become." Truth is, I work my butt off—in the field and at my computer. My advice is, "Work hard, get lucky!"

But it is a dream job, traveling around the planet, looking through my camera, and capturing a frozen moment in time. (It was a nightmare, however, when I was seasick in the Philippines, and a horror when I had heatstroke in Morocco. But I still wouldn't trade my job for anything—except maybe to play rhythm guitar for Eric Clapton or Carlos Santana.)

Image-making has evolved tremendously since I took pictures as a kid. Today, photography is really a 50-50 deal: 50 percent image capture, 50 percent digital darkroom work.

▲ FIGURE 1.2

Tech info: Canon EOS 1Ds Mark II, Canon 100-400mm IS lens @ 400mm. Exposure: 1/500 sec. @ f/8. ISO 800.

Make Pictures

There is a big difference between *taking* pictures and *making* pictures. My workshop co-leader, Darrell Gulin, and I made or set up or helped to set up most of the pictures in this section. That is, we worked with the subjects to get exactly the kind of pictures we envisioned in our minds.

This picture, like a scene from a wild-west movie, was totally set up (**Figure 1.2**). We picked the time of day. We picked the location for the backlit horses to ride out of a cloud of dust. We also selected the location for the photographers. Those directions yielded a picture that probably would be impossible to get by chance.

When you take the time to *make* pictures, you get photographs that go beyond a simple snapshot.

Think Creatively

When you're out in the field, use your imagination to compose pictures in your mind that others may not envision. To use the cliché, think outside the box—or frame.

This picture illustrates how a unique angle (shooting from ground level) and viewpoint (shooting between the legs of a cowboy) resulted in a creative photograph (**Figure 1.3**). This scene benefits from the fact that everything is in focus, from the cowboy's spurs to the building in the background. That's the result of using a very wide-angle lens set to a small aperture.

Fill the Frame

Here's one of my favorite photography tips: The name of the game is to fill the frame. When you fill the frame with the subject and/or subjects, you have less dead space in your picture. The less dead space, the more interesting the picture.

This picture illustrates another technique that I'll squeeze in (**Figure 1.4**). To get the entire scene in focus, use a wide-angle lens, focus one third of the way into the scene (using manual, not automatic, focus to get the greatest depth of field), and select a small aperture. Had I used a wider aperture or a longer lens and focused on the sleeping cowboy or the building, the entire scene would not have been in focus.

◀ FIGURE 1.3

Tech info: Canon EOS 1Ds Mark II, Canon 15mm lens. Exposure: 1/30 sec. @ f/11. ISO 100.

▲ FIGURE 1.4

Tech info: Canon EOS 1Ds Mark II, Canon 17-40mm lens @ 17mm. Exposure: 1/60 sec. @ f/11. ISO 100.

▲ FIGURE 1.5 and FIGURE 1.6 ▼

Tech info (for both figures): Canon EOS 1Ds Mark II, Canon 17-40mm lens @ 17mm. Exposure: 1/125 sec. @ f/8. ISO 100. A polarizing filter was used on the lens for both photographs to darken the blue sky and whiten the clouds.

Take Horizontal and Vertical Pictures

One of the first choices you have in taking a photograph is to shoot either a horizontal or a vertical picture. There is no right or wrong choice. However, if you follow the afore-mentioned tip about filling the frame, you'll quickly identify which format is more appropriate.

Speaking of filling the frame, you may think that I didn't fill the frame when taking these two pictures (**Figures 1.5** and **1.6**). However, the clouds added to the beauty of these scenes and illustrated "big sky country," so I chose to include them.

Provide a Sense of Place

I used to tell my photography students that the background was almost as important to me as the main subject. Today, I stress that the background *is as* important as the main subject because it gives the subject a sense of place.

▲ FIGURE 1.7

Tech info: Canon EOS 1Ds Mark II, Canon 28-105mm lens @ 100mm. Exposure: 1/250 sec. @ f/5.6. ISO 200.

▲ FIGURE 1.8

Tech info: Canon EOS 1Ds Mark II, Canon 28-105mm lens @ 35mm. Exposure: 1/125 sec. @ f/11. ISO 400.

For example, imagine how these cowboys (**Figures 1.7** and **1.8**) would look if I had photographed them in New York City or on a beach in Pago Pago.

When composing your pictures, pay careful attention to the background. If it's not right, you may have to move the subject to a new location. Or, if you can't work with the background you have, you could darken or blur it in Photoshop. You'd lose your sense of place, but you'd still have a nice picture.

Of course, you could also use Photoshop's Clone Stamp tool to remove distracting elements from the background, or even import a background from another image. But your best bet is to shoot with a good background in mind.

Look for Details

When you're composing a picture, look carefully—very carefully—at all the elements in a scene to see if they add or detract from the impact of your picture.

Check out the photograph of the cowboy (**Figure 1.9**). At first glance, it's a nice portrait. Look closer, and you'll see the reflection of the cowboy's horse in his sunglasses—a horse strategically positioned, by the way.

Now look at the picture of the cowgirl on the horse (**Figure 1.10**). What makes this picture interesting is the cowboy's shadow on the horse's rump. Here, I asked a cowboy to position himself that way. Little touches like that make the difference between a nice shot and a more creative image.

Tell a Story

In addition to being called a *light catcher*, you need to consider yourself a *storyteller*, because a successful photograph tells a story, as I mentioned at the beginning of this chapter (**Figure 1.11**).

To help you tell a story with a picture, try to write a caption for the picture in your mind while you're composing the scene. That process may help you with your composition and exposure. It may also tell you that you need to wait for just the right light, or add light with a flash or reflector, or diffuse light with a diffuser (**Figure 1.12**).

▲ FIGURE 1.9

Tech info: Canon EOS 1Ds Mark II, Canon 28-105mm lens @ 105mm. Exposure: 1/250 sec. @ f/8. ISO 400.

◄ FIGURE 1.10

Tech info: Canon EOS 1Ds Mark II, Canon 28-105mm lens @ 35mm. Exposure: 1/125 sec. @ f/8. ISO 100.

▲ FIGURE 1.11

Tech info: Canon EOS
1Ds Mark II, Canon 100-
400mm IS lens @ 300mm.
Exposure: 1/500 sec. @ f/8.
ISO 200.

◀ FIGURE 1.12

Tech info: Canon EOS
1Ds Mark II, Canon 100-
400mm IS lens @ 300mm.
Exposure: 1/500 sec. @ f/8.
ISO 200.

▶ FIGURE 1.13

Tech info: Canon EOS 1Ds Mark II, Canon 28-135mm IS lens @ 135mm. Exposure: 1/500 sec. @ f/8. ISO 400.

▶ FIGURE 1.14

Tech info: Canon EOS 1Ds Mark II, Canon 100-400mm IS lens @ 300mm. Exposure: 1/30 sec. @ f/8. ISO 200. A tripod was used to steady the camera.

Use Time to Your Advantage

Now let's look at two of my favorite pictures from the Double JJ Ranch. You can easily stop or blur the action in a photograph by adjusting the shutter speed on your camera. Slow shutter speeds (usually below 1/30 second) blur action; fast shutter speeds (usually above 1/500 second) stop or freeze it.

Both of these pictures say *action* in their own way, but the picture with the blurred background conveys a greater sense of speed (**Figures 1.13** and **1.14**). Sure, you can add a sense of speed to a picture using one of Photoshop's Blur filters; but, as always, it saves you time in your digital darkroom if you start with the picture that you see in your mind's eye. In addition to carefully selecting the aperture to get either all or part of a scene in focus, choose your shutter speed wisely.

Envision the End Result

Seeing pictures in the field is a part of the creative picture-taking process—a big part! But envisioning what can be done in Photoshop to enhance an image (covered in Chapter 2) and then adding an artistic touch to that image (covered in Chapters 3 and 4) is also important.

How do you get good at seeing? The same way you get good at any creative endeavor, such as playing the piano or guitar: practice.

When I was composing this picture of a herd of horses running toward me at top speed, I envisioned freezing the action and cropping out the top and bottom of the image so that the horses filled the frame (**Figure 1.15**). I also envisioned a black-and-white image (**Figure 1.16**), as well as a more artistic rendition created by applying Photoshop's Diffuse Glow filter (Filter > Distort > Diffuse Glow) to the image (**Figure 1.17**).

▼ FIGURES 1.15, 1.16, and 1.17

Tech info: Canon EOS 1Ds Mark II, Canon 100-400mm IS lens @ 200mm. Exposure: 1/500 sec. @ f/8. ISO 400.

Seeing More Possibilities with Photoshop

In the previous section, I touched on the value of *seeing* the finished image when looking through your camera's viewfinder. The visualizing process of seeing, or planning in advance, what can be done to an image in Photoshop CS2 is so important that I want to stress it by sharing a few more before-and-after examples. To illustrate my points, I'll use full-frame, unprocessed photographs (raw files) that I took during a once-in-a-lifetime Quark Expeditions (www.quarkexpeditions.com) adventure to Antarctica.

My goal in this section isn't to show any so-called *artistic* techniques—that is, applying special effects to an image. You'll see plenty of that later in this book. Rather, I'd like to show you how some basic Photoshop possibilities—enhancements that I saw in my mind's eye when I was composing the images—transformed already good pictures into more creative images. If you start out with a strong image, just imagine what you can do with it in Photoshop!

How do you "see" the end result? Well, having lots of experience taking pictures and working and playing in Photoshop helps. Talking to yourself, or rather, asking yourself when you're photographing if this or that technique would look cool, is another method (but don't talk out loud if you're in a group, or someone may think you're losing it).

Some of the following techniques, I admit, are simple. Often, however, when you keep it simple, that simplicity unlocks a new way of seeing—and thinking.

▼ FIGURE 1.18

Tech info: Canon EOS 1Ds Mark II, Canon 17-40mm lens @ 17mm. Exposure: 1/500 sec. @ f/11. ISO 100.

Compose the Scene

Let's begin with an image from my Antarctica adventure (**Figure 1.18**). I took the picture of an iceberg knowing that lens flare, created by direct light falling on the front element of the lens, was dominating the upper left of the frame and ruining, in my mind, a full-frame image. However, my goal was not a full-frame shot. Rather, I envisioned a panoramic image of the dramatic iceberg with much less sky. I had to compose the scene in this manner from a bobbing Zodiac inflatable boat to get the very wide-angle effect I envisioned.

What's more, I saw a black-and-white image rather than a color image. Why? Because I like the look of black-and-white images of monochrome landscape scenes, and all the blue in this scene created a monotone image anyway.

To create the black-and-white image, I went to Image > Adjustments > Hue/Saturation and completely desaturated the image (Command-U: Mac or Ctrl-U: Win) (Figure 1.19). (Even better, use an Adjustment Layer. See the sidebar "Adjustment Layers Are a Must!" in Chapter 2.)

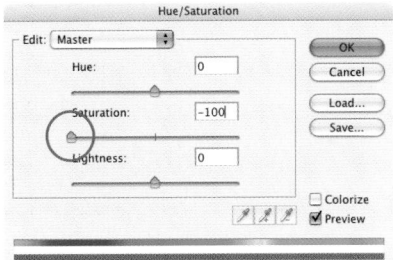

FIGURE 1.19

After I desaturated the image, it looked a little flat. I boosted the contrast by going to Image > Adjustments > Brightness/Contrast and moving the Contrast slider a little to the right (Figure 1.20).

Voilà! This is the image that appeared in my mind's eye when I first saw the magnificent natural ice sculpture (Figure 1.21).

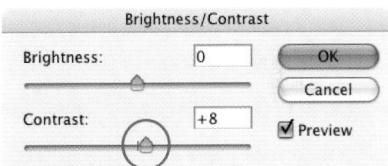

FIGURE 1.20

FIGURE 1.21

Here's a closer look at the same iceberg. At first glance, it looks like an OK picture (**Figure 1.22**). But wait!

Lens flare was still a problem, as you can see by the area I've outlined in the image (**Figure 1.23**). Come on. Be honest. Did you see it in the previous image? (By the way, digital SLR cameras are more susceptible to lens flare than film cameras, due to the reflectivity of the shiny image sensor: Light can bounce off the image sensor onto the rear element of the lens, causing flare.)

Here, too, I envisioned a tighter shot—a tight, square image (**Figure 1.24**)—and I think that this picture has more impact than the previous picture. I cropped the image using the Crop (press C: Mac or Win) tool, saved it, closed it, and then opened it again, for a reason you'll see shortly.

▼ FIGURE 1.22

Tech info: Canon EOS
1Ds Mark II, Canon
17-40mm lens @ 17mm.
Exposure: 1/500 sec.
@ f/5.6. ISO 100.

FIGURE 1.23

FIGURE 1.24

At this stage, the image looked a bit flat, so I went to Image > Adjustments > Brightness/Contrast to boost the contrast. Overall, the picture looks better (Figure 1.25). But the part of the ice that was strongly illuminated by the sun is now over-exposed—an expected result of my boosting the contrast. No problem.

FIGURE 1.25

I selected the History Brush from the Tool Bar (Figure 1.26) and "painted" back the detail in that area by going "back in time" to the unadjusted area of the picture. Keep in mind that had I cropped the picture after opening the image, I couldn't have used the History Brush, because it becomes inactive once a picture is cropped (unless you save a file, close it, and then reopen it).

As you can see in this image, the History Brush works wonders (Figure 1.27)!

FIGURE 1.27

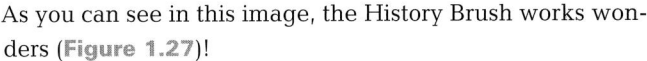

FIGURE 1.26

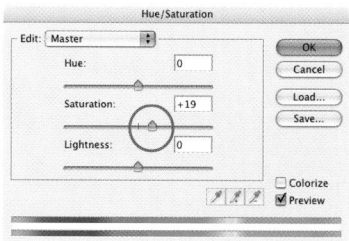

FIGURE 1.28

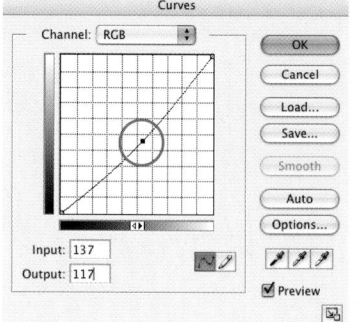

FIGURE 1.29

FIGURE 1.30

Here I wanted to maintain a full-color image. However, I wasn't satisfied with the color. So, I went to Image > Adjustments > Hue/Saturation and boosted the Saturation (**Figure 1.28**).

To increase the saturation even more and to make the image darker, I chose Image > Adjustments > Curves (Command-M: Mac or Ctrl-M: Win) and pulled down the Curves line from the center point (**Figure 1.29**).

Compare this image (**Figure 1.30**) to the first shot in this sequence. What do you think?

Here is another example of how you can use the History Brush to control contrast and brightness in a select area of an image (**Figures 1.31** and **1.32**). The picture that shows the overexposed breasts of the albatrosses was the result of increasing the contrast in a somewhat flat-looking image file. The properly exposed picture is the result of using the History Brush on the birds' breasts. That is the exposure I originally envisioned.

I took the picture of sea ice with a full-frame 15mm fisheye lens; when tilted up or down, this lens bends the horizon line (**Figure 1.33**). I wanted that exact effect when I saw this scene. (Standing in the near-freezing water was the hardest part of taking this picture.)

I thought the scene would have more impact as a black-and-white image, so I experimented with different methods for getting that result. In this case, I went to Image > Mode > Grayscale. (See Chapter 4 for detailed information on creating black-and-white images.)

Once again, here is the image I envisioned when I first saw this breathtaking scene (**Figure 1.34**).

▲ FIGURE 1.31 and FIGURE 1.32 ▶

Tech info: Canon EOS 1D Mark II, Canon 100-400mm lens @ 200 mm. Exposure: 1/250 sec. @ f/8. ISO 400.

▲ FIGURE 1.33

Tech info: Canon EOS 1Ds Mark II, Canon 15mm lens. Exposure: 1/250 sec. @ f/8. ISO 100.

FIGURE 1.34

▲ FIGURES 1.35, 1.36, 1.37

Tech info: Canon
EOS 1Ds Mark II, Canon
17-40mm lens @ 17mm.
Exposure: 1/500 sec. @
f/11. ISO 100.

It's a good idea to try to see pictures within a picture. In this set of images, you can see two additional pictures I envisioned within the original, wide-angle photograph (**Figures 1.35**, **1.36**, and **1.37**).

See the Color of Light

In addition to training your eyes to see the light (the highlights and contrast in a scene), you need to learn how to see the color of light. Warm light has deeper shades of red, yellow, and orange than cool light, which has a blue cast.

The picture of a leopard seal was taken on an overcast day when the light was flat and gray (Figure 1.38).

To warm up the picture, I chose Image > Adjustments > Photo Filter and applied Warming Filter (LBA) (Figure 1.39), adjusting the Density slider to suit my personal taste. As you can see, I cropped the picture a little for a square image (Figure 1.40).

▲ FIGURE 1.38

Tech info: Canon EOS 1D Mark II, Canon 100-400mm lens @ 200 mm. Exposure: 1/250 sec. @ f/8. ISO 400.

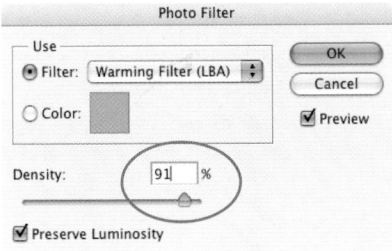

FIGURE 1.39

FIGURE 1.40

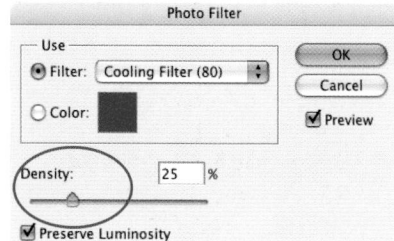

FIGURE 1.41

TIP: For a perfect square, hold down the Shift key when using the Crop tool.

To achieve the opposite effect—cooling off the image—I applied the Cooling Filter (80) (**Figure 1.41**), again adjusting the Density slider to taste (**Figure 1.42**).

Have Fun with Frames and Type

Envisioning the post-photography fun as well as the creative options that you can have in Photoshop is important. Part of that enjoyment can involve adding digital frames to a picture, and Photoshop offers some cool built-in digital frames.

When you compose a picture in-camera, it is usually a good idea to shoot tight and fill the frame with the main subject. However, if you plan to add certain types of frames to the image, you may want to leave some space around the edges.

TIP: Frames are included with Photoshop's built-in Actions. To load them, click the little fly-out arrow at the top right of the Actions dialog box. Then, click Frames in the pop-up menu.

On the next page are examples of the Drop Shadow (**Figure 1.43**) and Photo Corners frames (**Figure 1.44**).

FIGURE 1.42

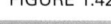

FIGURE 1.43

FIGURE 1.44

FIGURE 1.45

And speaking of fun, when I'm in the field shooting, I often think about sharing my pictures with family, friends, and business associates. I compose a picture and add type to create an e-card (which is a low-resolution JPEG image with type embedded). Here's an e-card that I created on site, using onOne Software's PhotoFrame 2.5 (**Figure 1.45**); I send it to busy folks who don't return my phone calls.

It pays to think before you shoot. Get practicing. See and picture your world in your own unique way.

Real Artists Shoot Raw
(But Don't Panic If You Shoot JPEGs)

"Raw Rules" is a favorite chant during the digital photography workshops that I teach. My students, after learning about the power of shooting raw files combined with the tremendous capabilities of processing the files in Camera Raw, and after seeing what they have been missing by shooting JPEG images, adopt the "Raw Rules" chant with enthusiasm—swearing they will never again shoot JPEG files for their serious shots.

For those JPEG shooters who haven't yet converted to the raw side (again, just for serious shots), this sidebar explains the top reasons to shoot raw files. I've also included some interesting stuff about shooting raw files and

processing them in Camera Raw—because processing a raw file, also called a *digital negative*, is an equally important step in getting a good final image.

First, however, I will say that there is a time and place to shoot a JPEG file. Because raw files take up much more memory than JPEG files, JPEG files may be preferred when memory card and hard drive space is limited. JPEG files can also be written to a memory card faster than raw files; when you're shooting an action sequence, a camera's buffer may fill up after shooting several raw files, due to their large size. When you're photographing a scene without strong highlights and shadows, a large JPEG

FIGURE 1.46

file may produce just as nice a print (up to a point) as a raw file. Finally, my guess is that a wedding photographer who shoots 500 or 600 pictures a day may not want to shoot raw files and then have to process all of them—although doing so is relatively easy, especially if your computer has lots of RAM.

Don't panic! If you shoot JPEG files or have lots of old JPEGs stuffed in folders on accessory hard drives, CDs, or DVDs, you can still use all the lessons in this book. Once you open a raw file in Photoshop CS2, processing is the same (except that you may have to change a 16-bit image to an 8-bit image [Image > Mode > 8 Bits] to access *all* of Photoshop CS2's functions, including some filters). But I recommend that you start, like all true artists, with the best possible tools at your fingertips.

To illustrate this lesson, I'll use some pictures that I took on one of my photography work-shops at the Double JJ Ranch (**Figure 1.46**). I'll also share a few screen grabs from the Camera Raw dialog box. And speaking of the Camera Raw dialog box, that's where you process, and take total control of, the raw file. Get to know it. It can be your friend!

Now, let's take a look at why Raw Rules. I've also included a few fun facts about raw files and Camera Raw that may be new to you:

◆ JPEG files toss away a third or more of the image data, without even asking you. Can you imagine what that trashing does to your image? That's right: The image gets trashed. Raw files contain more image data than JPEG files, which is important when you want to capture the fine details in a scene, such as

this beautiful cowgirl's freckles and eyelashes (**Figure 1.47**).

Processing raw files in Camera Raw is less destructive to an image than processing a JPEG image in Photoshop CS2 because you're working in a 16-bit mode. The more bits an image file contains, the better the quality will be. It's similar to the situation faced by film photographers: If a landscape image shot with 35mm film looks OK, it will look great when photographed on 4x5 sheet film.

◆ JPEG files are already processed when they come out of your camera, with color, sharp-ness, and other enhancements applied. With a raw file, you get the raw image that you can process to your heart's content. The only data applied to your image in-camera are the ISO, f-stop, and shutter speed. For scenes like this, where oversharpening and oversaturation (especially of the red tones in the cowboy's shirt) could cause a loss of detail, I prefer not to let the camera set the file's sharpness, con-trast, and saturation (**Figure 1.48**).

FIGURE 1.47   FIGURE 1.48

- Raw files have a wider exposure latitude than JPEG files, so they're more forgiving of your exposures. That's cool when you're shooting high-contrast scenes or scenes with bright highlights, such as the sand on the beach of this small island (**Figure 1.49**).

FIGURE 1.49

- Camera Raw has the amazing ability to recover overexposed areas of a scene—sometimes a full f-stop. That's helpful when you're photographing scenes like this in which the white on the horses may be a bit overexposed (**Figure 1.50**).
- The histogram on your camera's LCD monitor isn't the histogram for the raw image, but for a JPEG version of that image. Judge your exposure accordingly.
- The overexposure warning on your camera isn't for the raw image. Again, it's for a JPEG version of that image.
- The highlight and shadow clipping warnings in Camera Raw make it easy for you to see what areas of an image are or will be washed out (shown in red) or lost in the shadows (shown in blue) (**Figures 1.51** and **1.52**). (Because I didn't have an incorrectly exposed picture from my trip, I simulated the over- and underexposure effects in Camera Raw to illustrate the clipping warnings.)

FIGURE 1.50

FIGURE 1.51

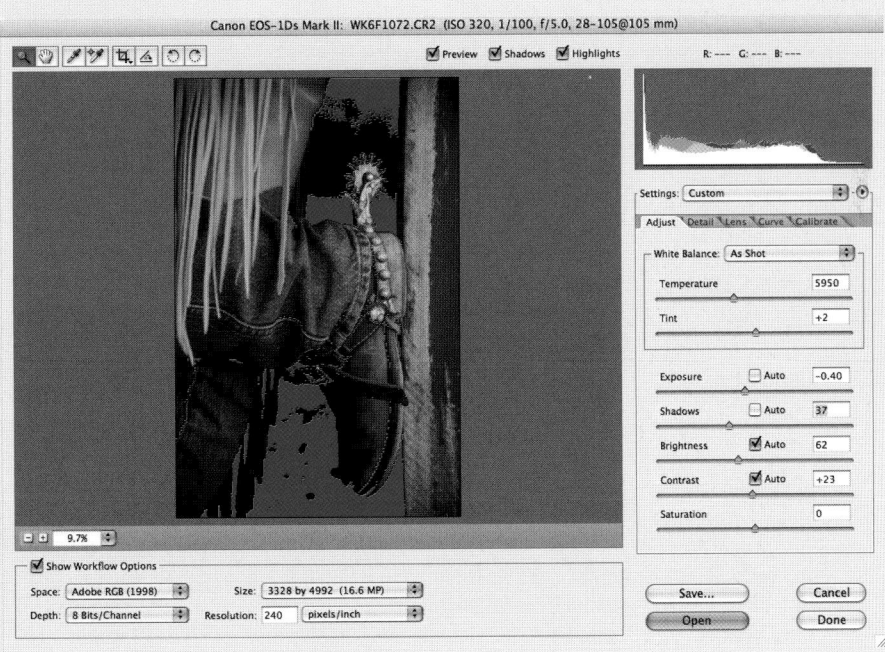

FIGURE 1.52

FIGURE 1.53

See? I did get a good exposure of the cow-girl's boot and spurs (which is a top stock photography seller, by the way) (**Figure 1.53**).

◆ You can easily correct and adjust all of the following using the Camera Raw plug-in: exposure, white balance, contrast, saturation, brightness, tint, chromatic aberrations, luminance, color noise, sharpness, and vignetting. You can even calibrate Camera Raw to your camera. Shown here are the dialog boxes for the Adjust, Detail, Lens, Curve, and Calibrate tabs (**Figures 1.54** through **1.58**).

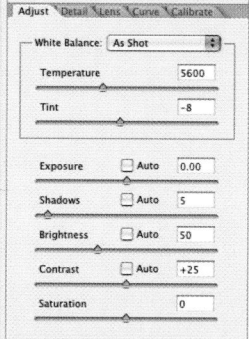

FIGURE 1.54

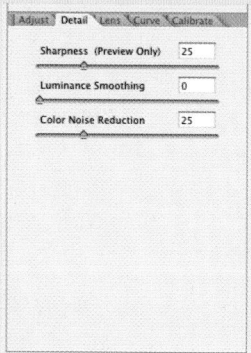

FIGURE 1.55

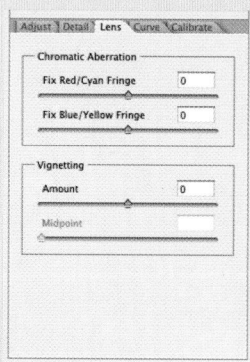

FIGURE 1.56

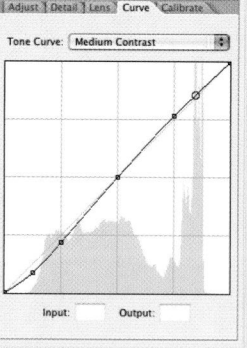

FIGURE 1.57

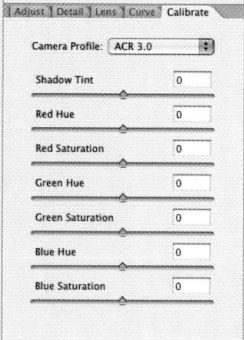

FIGURE 1.58

- Camera Raw, in conjunction with Adobe Photoshop CS2 and Adobe Bridge, makes finding, processing, and enhancing pictures super easy—and fun!

My guess is that you now agree: Raw Rules! However, it's as important as ever to start with the best possible in-camera image and to carefully select the subject and compose the scene, two of the most important elements in photography. This picture of cowboys herding horses is one of my favorites from my Michigan workshop (**Figure 1.59**). Believe it or not, the image needed little image processing, because I followed my own picture-taking advice.

FIGURE 1.59

2 Image-Enhancement Artistry

WE'RE ALL ARTISTS, creative individuals who use the tools at our disposal to create unique images. As digital photographers, we have two creative tools: our camera and Photoshop. In my workshops, I say that today, photography is a 50-50 deal: 50 percent image capture, 50 percent Photoshop. Photoshop lets you use your creativity and imagination to transform your images into works of art. With a few clicks of a mouse or taps of a stylus, you can give your pictures more impact and correct mistakes in composition and exposure. These aren't new tricks. Traditional "wet" darkroom artists have been using techniques to accomplish these goals almost since the beginning of photography.

In this chapter, we'll look at some basic artistic image enhancements. I've chosen pictures—a wildlife shot, a landscape, a portrait, an outdoor action scene, and an indoor low-light scene—that are typical of photographs you probably have. When reading this chapter and looking at my examples, keep your own pictures in mind and try to visualize how you can transform them.

LET'S EXPLORE!

Jump into Easy Image Enhancements

▼ FIGURE 2.1

Tech info: Canon EOS 1D Mark II, Canon 28-105mm lens @ 50mm. Exposure: 1/500 sec. @ f/8. ISO 400.

Question: Do you know the difference between a professional photographer and an amateur?

Answer: A pro never has to show his or her outtakes.

Although that photographer joke is mostly true, I thought I'd share one of my outtakes with you, with the goal of illustrating how easy it is to turn an outtake into a keeper.

My original shot of a horse and rider has a few problems: It's lopsided, there's too much dead space, the colors are dull, you can't see the rider's face clearly, and the dark horse looks, well, too dark (**Figure 2.1**). Other than that, it's a great shot!

I made a copy of the original so I could work on the copy. My first step was to crop and straighten the image (**Figure 2.2**).

In Photoshop, an easy way to straighten an image is to go to Filter> Distort > Lens Correction and then rotate the Angle (by clicking the line inside the wheel) until your image is straight (**Figure 2.3**).

In the same window, you can also straighten an image by using the Straighten tool. Select the tool, drag it along a level line in the scene, and then release your mouse (or stylus) (**Figure 2.4**).

If you're working in Camera Raw (which I always do first), you can use the Straighten tool (press A: Mac or Win) in the same manner just described. Doing so crops and straightens the image.

FIGURE 2.2

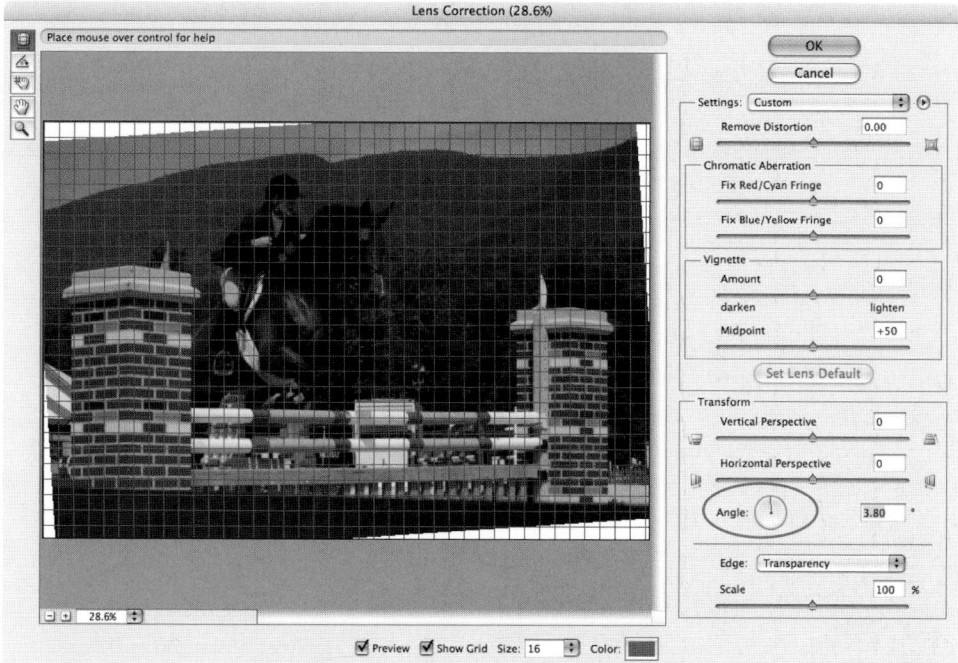

FIGURE 2.3

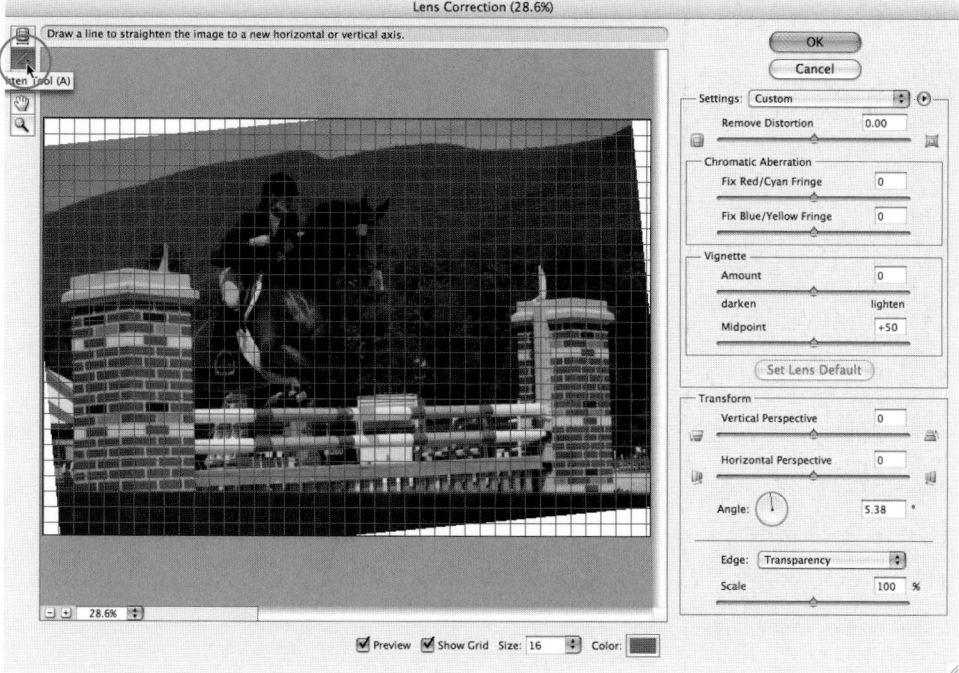

FIGURE 2.4

Next, I duplicated the image by clicking it in the Layers palette (where it's called Background, in this case) and dragging it down to the "Create a new layer" icon at the bottom of the palette. Then, I created a Layer Mask by clicking the "Add a mask" icon (**Figure 2.5**). The Layer Mask is the white box next to the image (**Figure 2.6**). Layer Masks let you apply and undo an effect quickly and easily.

My goal at this stage of the process was to see into (lighten) the shadow areas, including the rider's face and the horse's body. In the Layers palette, on the top layer, I clicked the picture of the horse and rider—not the Layer Mask. I selected Shadow/Highlight (Image > Adjustments > Shadow/ Highlight), moved the Shadows sliders until I was pleased with what the shadow areas revealed (**Figure 2.7**), and then clicked OK. (If your Shadow/Highlight window doesn't include all the options shown here, click Show More Options at the bottom of the window.) The other areas of the image were too light at this point, but that's where the Layer Mask's utility came in handy.

Next, I clicked my Layer Mask on the top layer (**Figure 2.8**).

I selected the Brush tool and a soft airbrush (because I wanted soft edges) (**Figure 2.9**). With my foreground color set to black (the front box at

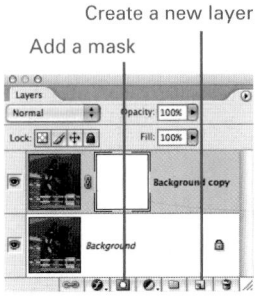

FIGURE 2.5

FIGURE 2.6

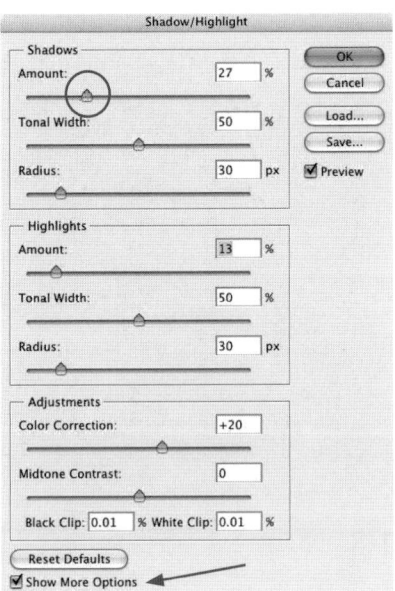

FIGURE 2.7

the bottom of the Tool Bar), I clicked inside the image and "painted back" areas of the picture I didn't want to lighten—everything except the horse's body and the rider's face. When I made a mistake, accidentally moving the eraser over the horse or the rider's face, I pressed the X key on my keyboard to switch the foreground/background colors and painted out the effect with white. You can also click the double-ended, curved arrow to change the foreground and background colors.

In **Figure 2.10**, taken from the working image window with the Background layer turned off, you see the effect of my erasing using the Layer Mask. I need to be a bit more careful with my erasing. To see how well you're erasing, turn off the Background layer by clicking the eye icon on that layer in the Layers palette.

Next, I wanted to sharpen the key elements in the picture: the horse and rider. To do so, I applied the Unsharp Mask filter (Filter > Sharpen > Unsharp Mask) to the image (not the Layer Mask) on the top layer (**Figure 2.11**). That sharpened only the horse and rider and not the background, due to my layer and Layer Mask setup.

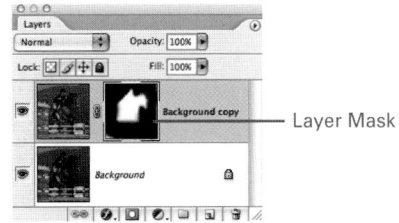

Layer Mask

FIGURE 2.8

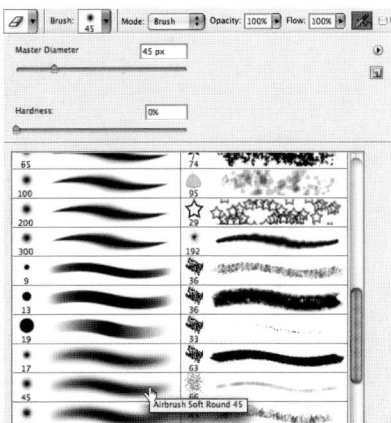

FIGURE 2.9

FIGURE 2.10

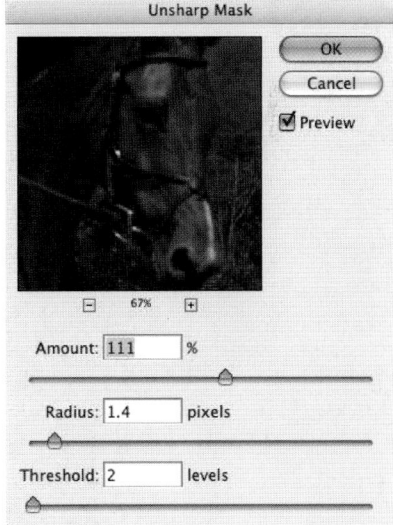

FIGURE 2.11

TIP: I always think selectively about sharpening (and most other image enhancements). For example, imagine this horse and rider jumping in the air against a sky background. There would be no reason to sharpen the sky; doing so might increase the digital noise in the sky. Plus, most people prefer a soft sky in a picture.

After those enhancements, I flattened the image (after saving a copy with the layers intact) because I wanted to send it to Peachpit Press for inclusion in this book. Then, I took a break and played a bit of electric guitar while listening to my iTunes.

When I came back to the flattened image, I realized that more enhancements could improve it. I increased the contrast (Layer > New Adjustment Layer > Brightness/Contrast) and boosted the saturation (Layer > New Adjustment Layer > Hue/Saturation). I also used the Burn tool (press O: Mac or Win) to darken the white poles in the picture and the Dodge tool to lighten the rider's face a little more. Finally, to dress up the image, I added a black border around it.

To do that, I selected a small area inside the frame by using the Rectangular Marquee tool, reversed the selection (Select > Inverse, or Shift-Command-I: Mac or Shift-Ctrl-I: Win) and then filled the newly selected area with black (Edit > Fill, and select Black from the Use pop-up menu) (**Figure 2.12**). When filling a selection, you have several options: Black, White, Foreground Color, and so on. Click Use in the Fill window to see these options.

I also made two more changes. Can you tell what they are? Take a close look (**Figure 2.13**). Using the Clone Stamp tool (press S: Mac or Win), I removed the dead tree from next to the horse's face and the red flag from atop the post.

Now it's your turn to jump into some easy image enhancements.

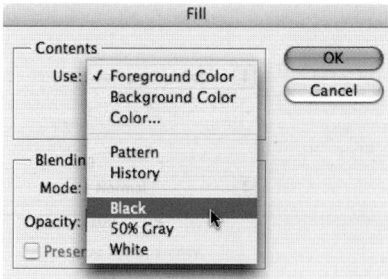

FIGURE 2.12

FIGURE 2.13

Let the Sun Shine In

Here's an example of how you can turn a cloudy day into a sunny day, for an image with more impact.

I took this picture of several dancers at a festival in Bhutan (**Figure 2.14**). Due to the overcast sky, the picture is flat. But let's see what happens with a little Photoshop magic.

▲ FIGURE 2.14

Tech info: Canon EOS 1Ds Mark II, Canon 17-40mm lens @ 17mm. Exposure: 1/500 sec. @ f/8. ISO 400.

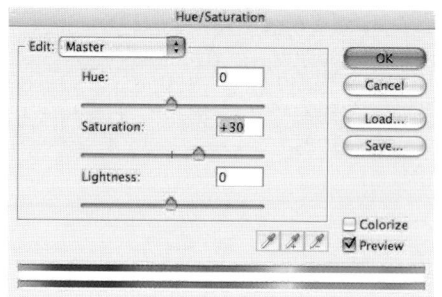

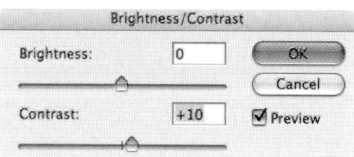

FIGURE 2.16

FIGURE 2.15

I first went to Layer > New Adjustment Layer > Hue/Saturation and boosted the Saturation to +30 (**Figure 2.15**).

Next, I chose Layer > New Adjustment Layer > Brightness/Contrast and boosted the Contrast to +10 (**Figure 2.16**).

Now the picture looks as though it were taken on a sunny day (**Figure 2.17**). That was easy!

FIGURE 2.17

▲ FIGURE 2.18

Tech info: Canon EOS 1D Mark II, Canon 100-400mm IS lens @ 400mm. Exposure: 1/500 sec. @ f/8. ISO 400.

Draw Attention to a Subject

Renaissance artists used a simple technique to draw the viewer's attention to the main subject in their paintings: They applied darker oils around the edges of the scene, leaving the subject in the brighter area.

You can simulate that effect in your photographs with Photoshop—and you don't have to be Rembrandt.

Here's how I used the edge-darkening technique to enhance a picture of a leopard I took in Botswana (**Figure 2.18**). I could have used the Burn tool (press O: Mac or Win) to darken the edges, but that approach would have taken a long time (and it would have been difficult to burn the edges evenly). The following method is easier and provides an even burn around the edges.

I first selected the Elliptical Marquee tool (press M: Mac or Win) (**Figure 2.19**), clicked inside the image, and created an oval around the main subject (**Figure 2.20**).

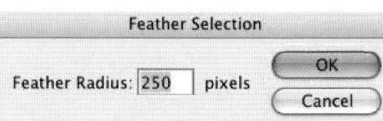

FIGURE 2.21

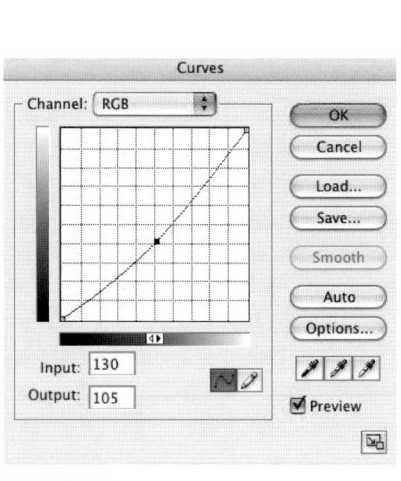

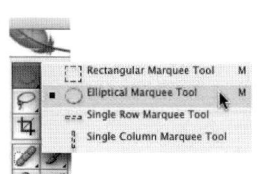

FIGURE 2.19

FIGURE 2.20

FIGURE 2.22

Next, I chose Select > Inverse to select the area outside the oval. That's the area that will eventually be darkened.

I chose Select > Feather to bring up the Feather Selection dialog box. For my 300 ppi, 5x7-inch picture, I selected a Feather Radius of 250 because I wanted a very, very gradual transition between the darkened area and the untouched area (**Figure 2.21**).

Now it was time to evenly darken the edges of the picture. I went to Layer > New Adjustment Layer > Curves and pulled down the curve from the center of the grid until I was pleased with the effect (**Figure 2.22**). (If you're in CMYK mode rather than RGB mode, you need to pull the curve *up*.)

Here's how my leopard photograph was enhanced using this technique—with a little extra help from the Burn tool, which I used to darken the out-of-focus twigs in the foreground (**Figure 2.23**).

FIGURE 2.23

Enhance Landscapes

The late Ansel Adams, a film photographer who was considered a landscape artist, was among the first to admit that the traditional wet darkroom played a very important role in his work—transforming seemingly dull negatives and test prints into photographs that look almost three-dimensional and have rich tones. Today, in the digital darkroom, you can create the same traditional darkroom effects achieved by Mr. Adams, plus many more.

▲ FIGURE 2.24

Tech info: Canon EOS 1Ds Mark II, Canon 17-40mm lens @ 17mm. Exposure: 1/125 sec. @ f/16. ISO 100.

In this lesson, I'll show you how I used Photoshop to transform a lackluster landscape picture taken in Arches National Park in Utah (**Figure 2.24**).

Levels (Layer > New Adjustment Layer > Levels) is a good place to start image enhancements (although many pros like to use Curves). Levels gives you a tremendous amount of creative control over the brightness, contrast, and color of your image. The histogram, or "mountain range," in the Levels dialog box shows that this image lacks some shadows (the flat part where the mountain range ends on the left side of the histogram) and some highlights (the flat part where the mountain range ends on the right) (**Figure 2.25**).

You can make a basic Levels adjustment to enhance shadow and highlight areas by moving the slider arrows inside the mountain range in the histogram (**Figure 2.26**). I usually experiment with different slider positions to see how they affect my image.

Here's the result of correcting the photograph's Levels (**Figure 2.27**). Now the image has more color and contrast. Cool!

But speaking of cool, I took the picture around mid-day, when the light was cool; as a result, the image has a slightly blue cast. (I wanted to photograph this scene in the late afternoon, but I was on the move and had to get to another location.) So, I created late-afternoon lighting: a warmer quality of light with deeper shades of red and yellow.

In the Hue/Saturation dialog box (Layer > New Adjustment Layer > Hue/Saturation), I boosted the Saturation and then clicked OK (**Figure 2.28**). How much you increase the Saturation is a matter of personal choice.

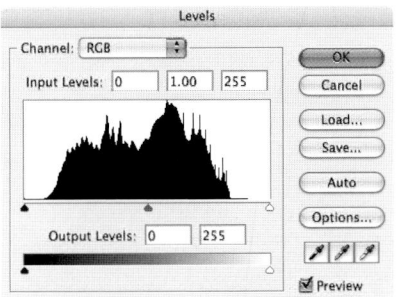

FIGURE 2.25

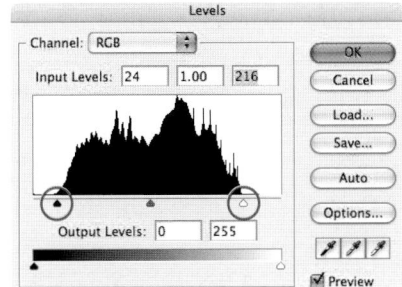

FIGURE 2.26

▼ FIGURE 2.27

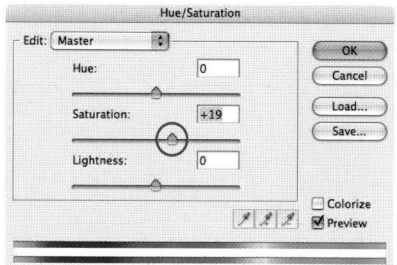

FIGURE 2.28

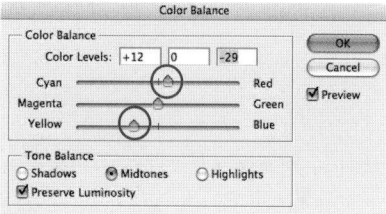

FIGURE 2.29

In the Color Balance dialog box (Layer > New Adjustment Layer > Color Balance), I increased the Red and Yellow tones (**Figure 2.29**). Again, it's your call as to how much you want to modify these tones.

You aren't done yet! Landscape photographers, whether they work in the wet or digital darkroom, often darken the edges of a picture to draw more attention to the main subject in the center of the frame—as I did earlier with the leopard photo. That's easy to do in Photoshop.

Using the Rectangular Marquee tool, I selected an area an inch or so into the frame. A dotted white line showed the selected area—the part inside the line (**Figure 2.30**).

I then chose Select > Inverse (press Shift-Command-I: Mac or Shift-Ctrl-I: Win) to invert the selection. Now the area *outside* the dotted white line was selected.

For a smooth transition from the darkened edges to the main part of the image, I went to Select > Feather, and in the Feather Selection dialog box, I chose a Feather Radius of 200 (**Figure 2.31**). That value worked well for my 300 ppi, 5×7-inch image. Your Feather Radius will depend on your personal taste and the image resolution.

Finally, to darken the selected area, I went to Levels and moved the Shadow triangle on the slider bar to the right. As

FIGURE 2.30

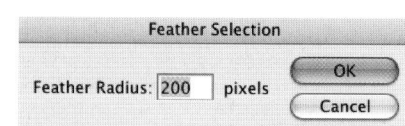

FIGURE 2.31

FIGURE 2.32

always, how much you move it depends on your personal taste. My goal was to make the edges darker, but not to the point that they were distracting. As you can see, the edges of the picture are evenly darkened (**Figure 2.32**).

If you want to try to emulate the works of Ansel Adams, you can convert your color image to black and white (**Figure 2.33**). See the section "Black-and-White and Beyond" in Chapter 4 for ideas on how to do that.

When you're photographing landscapes, keep in mind the creative enhancements that are possible in Photoshop and how much fun you can have transforming your images.

FIGURE 2.33

Saving Face

Like landscape photographer Ansel Adams, master portrait photographer Yousef Karsh was open about the fact that much of his artistry was achieved in the darkroom. (If you aren't familiar with the work of Karsh, also known as Karsh of Ottawa, do a Web search and learn more about one of the greatest portrait photographers of all time.)

You can use many of the techniques Karsh and other film-based photographers used in their wet darkrooms to enhance your digital portraits of people and animals. In this lesson, we'll look at just a few of the enhancements possible using Photoshop.

We'll begin with a picture of a sexy senior citizen I photographed in Italy. The straight-out-of-the-camera shot is too saturated and a bit dark (**Figure 2.34**).

NOTE: *Skilled Photoshop folks: Don't panic that I'm not using a Layer Mask for this technique. I know you know that the following technique is often said to be destructive. However, it's easier to understand than using a Layer Mask. What's more, I've used this technique, and some of the resulting images appear in my books—and I haven't seen any difference in the two approaches. I'm also not using Adjustment Layers, to get the point across more quickly. But yes, they are a must, as I stress in a moment.*

As a first step, I reduced the Saturation by going to Hue/Saturation (**Figure 2.35**).

▼ FIGURE 2.34

Tech info: Canon EOS 1Ds Mark II, Canon 28-135mm IS lens @ 10mm. Exposure: 1/125 sec. @ f/5.6. ISO 640.

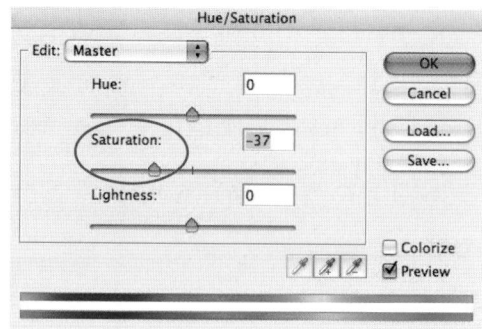

FIGURE 2.35

My portrait was now more pleasing, but the man's face was still dark and flat (Figure 2.36).

I wanted to isolate the man's face from the rest of the scene, so I made a duplicate layer by dragging the original layer to the "Create a new layer" icon at the bottom of the Layers palette (Figure 2.37). I turned off the top layer by clicking the eye icon next to it in the Layers palette and then clicking the bottom layer to activate it (Figure 2.38). That was now my working layer.

To brighten the man's face, I went to Levels and moved the Highlight slider to the left, just inside the mountain range (which shows the distribution of the highlights and shadows in a scene) (Figure 2.39).

Still working on the bottom layer, I went to Brightness/Contrast (using an Adjustment Layer, of course) and boosted Contrast a bit (Figure 2.40).

FIGURE 2.36

FIGURE 2.37

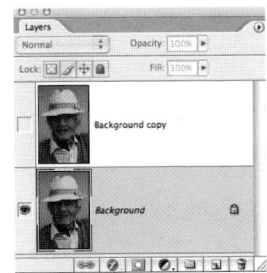

FIGURE 2.38

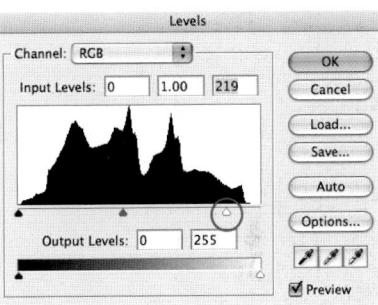

FIGURE 2.39

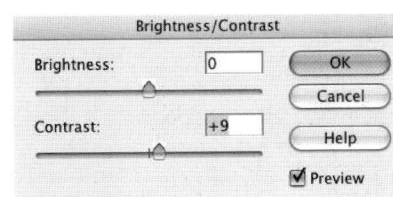

FIGURE 2.40

FIGURE 2.41

I was happy with the enhancements to the man's face, so I selected the top layer in the Layers palette for the next step (**Figure 2.41**). I used the Eraser tool (press E: Mac or Win) to erase the man's face. **Figure 2.42** shows the area I erased; the face is blank because I turned off the bottom layer (by clicking the eye icon). That's a good way to see whether you're doing a good job of erasing.

Here are the results of my enhancements (**Figure 2.43**).

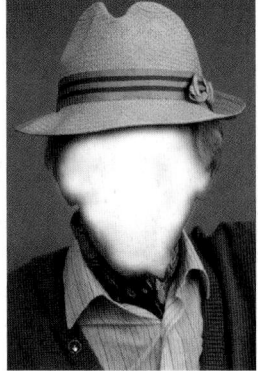

FIGURE 2.42

FIGURE 2.43 ▶

FIGURE 2.44

FIGURE 2.45

You may be wondering, "Why go through all the trouble of making a layer and clicking this layer and that layer when you could have used Levels and the other controls to enhance the entire picture?" The next image shows the answer.

Had I made the enhancements to the entire image, the highlight areas (the bright areas of the man's straw hat and his shirt) would have been blown out (overexposed) (**Figure 2.44**). The message is this: Use layers to isolate the part of the image you want to enhance.

A while ago, I had the color picture of the man posted on my Web site. I received many emails from folks saying that they loved the man's face, but they wished I had posted a black-and-white version of the image. For those of you who feel the same way, here's the picture in black and white (**Figure 2.45**). (See the section "Black-and-White and Beyond" in Chapter 4 for more on how to create black-and-white images from your color files.)

Enter the Layer Mask

Let's look at another example of enhancements you can make to draw more attention to a subject's face—in this case, when the background is distracting. As in the first section of this chapter, I used a Layer Mask: a nondestructive image-enhancement technique. It's more advanced, but it offers the added benefit of letting you undo any mistakes quickly and easily rather than going to the History palette and clicking a previous step to undo an error.

Why did I show you the other technique in the previous section? Some folks have a hard time understanding Layer Masks, as I mentioned, and I figured I'd show you the basic concept before presenting one that's more difficult.

▼ FIGURE 2.46

Tech info: Canon EOS 1D Mark II, Canon 100-400mm IS lens @ 400mm. Exposure: 1/250 sec. @ f/8. ISO 800.

When I photographed this leopard at the Ft. Worth Zoo in Ft. Worth, Texas, I underexposed the file by one f-stop so as not to overexpose the white hairs on the animal's face (**Figure 2.46**). And the background is distracting—especially the foliage in the circled area, which looks like extra hairs protruding from the animal's face. ("Be aware of the background" is a good photo tip to follow, as noted in Chapter 1.)

After cropping the picture, I corrected the exposure by adjusting the Levels. I moved the Shadow and Highlight sliders to just inside the edges of the mountain range of the histogram (a basic Photoshop Levels enhancement) (**Figure 2.47**).

I wanted to soften the background using the Gaussian Blur filter. To control which area of the file was blurred, I first made a duplicate layer (by dragging the background layer to the "Create a new layer" icon at the bottom of the Layers palette). I clicked the top layer and then clicked the "Add a mask" icon at the bottom of the Layers palette (**Figure 2.48**).

Next, I applied the Gaussian Blur filter (Filter > Blur > Gaussian Blur) to the image area (the square on the left, not the Layer Mask) on the top layer (**Figure 2.49**). I then clicked the Layer Mask (the square on the right) on the top layer.

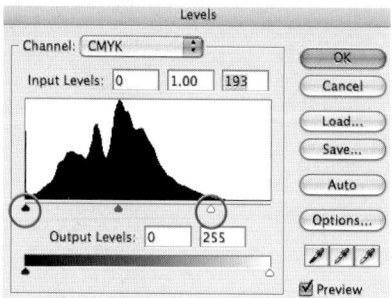

FIGURE 2.47

If this sounds confusing, remember that you want to apply the effect or enhancement to the image icon in the Layers palette (click it to activate it)—not to the Layer Mask icon beside it.

With my foreground color set to black and the background set to white (the default settings), I selected an airbrush from the Tool Bar and began painting out the blur over the leopard's face and body. If I erased into the background, I switched the background/foreground colors (by pressing X on the keyboard) and painted back in the blurred area with white. (This is a standard Layer Mask retouching technique.) Finally, I used the Clone Stamp tool to remove the most distracting branches from the background. Here's the end result (**Figure 2.50**).

The next time you see a face you want to photograph, think about how you can save it and/or make it more prominent in your picture.

FIGURE 2.48

FIGURE 2.49

FIGURE 2.50

Only the Shadows Know

Our eyes have the amazing ability to see a dynamic range of about eleven f-stops. That's why, in a high-contrast situation, such as viewing the magnificent ceiling of this cathedral, we can see details in the shadow areas without the highlight areas being washed out (**Figure 2.51**).

However, images that are straight out of the camera—even raw files—don't reveal the same dynamic range that our eyes can see. When I opened the raw file of my picture in Photoshop, the scene looked like this: It had virtually no shadow detail and had overexposed highlights (the windows) (**Figure 2.52**).

▼ FIGURE 2.51

Tech info: Canon EOS 1Ds Mark II, Canon 17-40mm lens @ 17mm. Exposure: 1/60 sec. @ f/4. ISO 200.

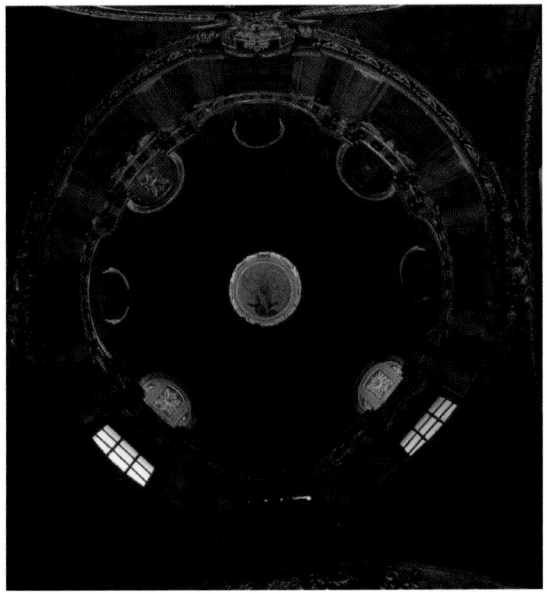

FIGURE 2.52

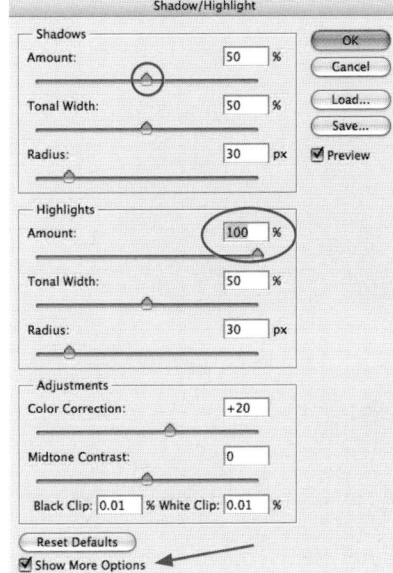

FIGURE 2.53

I knew the image would look like that, because I had exposed mostly for the highlights in order to preserve as much of the detail in the windows as possible. Sure, I could have underexposed the scene a bit more to preserve all the detail in the windows, but doing so would have resulted in a severely underexposed image, which, in turn, would have meant too much noise (grain) in the shadow areas.

Shadow/Highlight to the rescue!

Selecting Shadow/Highlight (Image > Adjustments > Shadow/Highlight) opens, that's right, the Shadow/Highlight dialog box. You'll need to click Show More Options at the bottom left in the window to see all the controls, as shown (Figure 2.53).

To adjust the image, I moved the Shadows Amount slider to 50% (which opened up the shadows) and the Highlights Amount slider to 100% (which toned down the highlights). These aren't magic numbers; you should gradually move the sliders to find the results you like best.

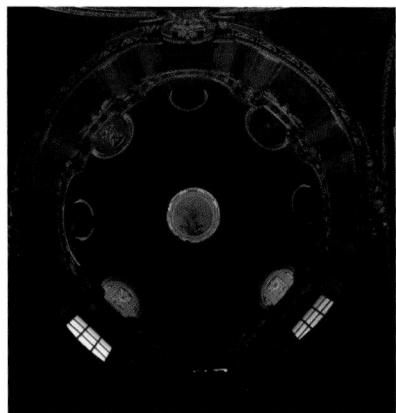

FIGURE 2.54

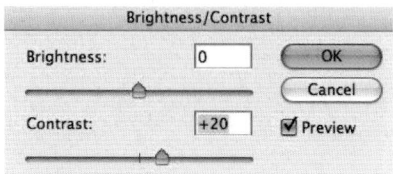

FIGURE 2.55

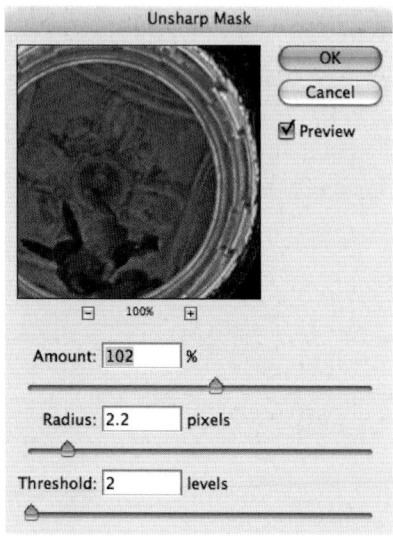

FIGURE 2.56

After making the Shadow/Highlight adjustment, my image looked like this—better, but still a bit flat (**Figure 2.54**).

To boost the contrast, I went to Layer > New Adjustment Layer > Brightness/Contrast and moved the Contrast slider in a positive direction until I saw something that looked good (**Figure 2.55**).

The picture still looked a little flat. So, I went to Filter > Sharpen > Unsharp Mask and increased the Amount to 102% (**Figure 2.56**). To see the successful result of this process, check out the opening picture in this lesson again. (In case you're wondering, I'm saving Photoshop's Smart Sharpen feature for my next book. It offers more control over sharpening, but for this example, Unsharp Mask is OK.)

You can also use Shadow/Highlight on your outdoor pictures. Here's a before-and-after example of how I used this adjustment to open up the shadows in the beach scene on the next page (**Figures 2.57** and **2.58**).

When you're looking at a scene that has strong shadows, keep Photoshop's Shadow/Highlight adjustment in mind, and expose the scene accordingly.

Color negative film can capture about seven f-stops, and color slide film can capture about three f-stops. Digital imaging rules, because you can save so much in the highlight areas and rescue so much in the shadow areas, especially if you shoot using your camera's raw format.

NOTE: If you didn't get the title of this lesson, it's a play on the famous line "Only the Shadow knows" from the old-time (1930–1954) mystery radio show, "The Shadow."

▶ FIGURES 2.57 and 2.58

Tech info: Canon EOS 1Ds Mark II, 15mm lens. Exposure: 1/125 sec. @ f/16. ISO 100.

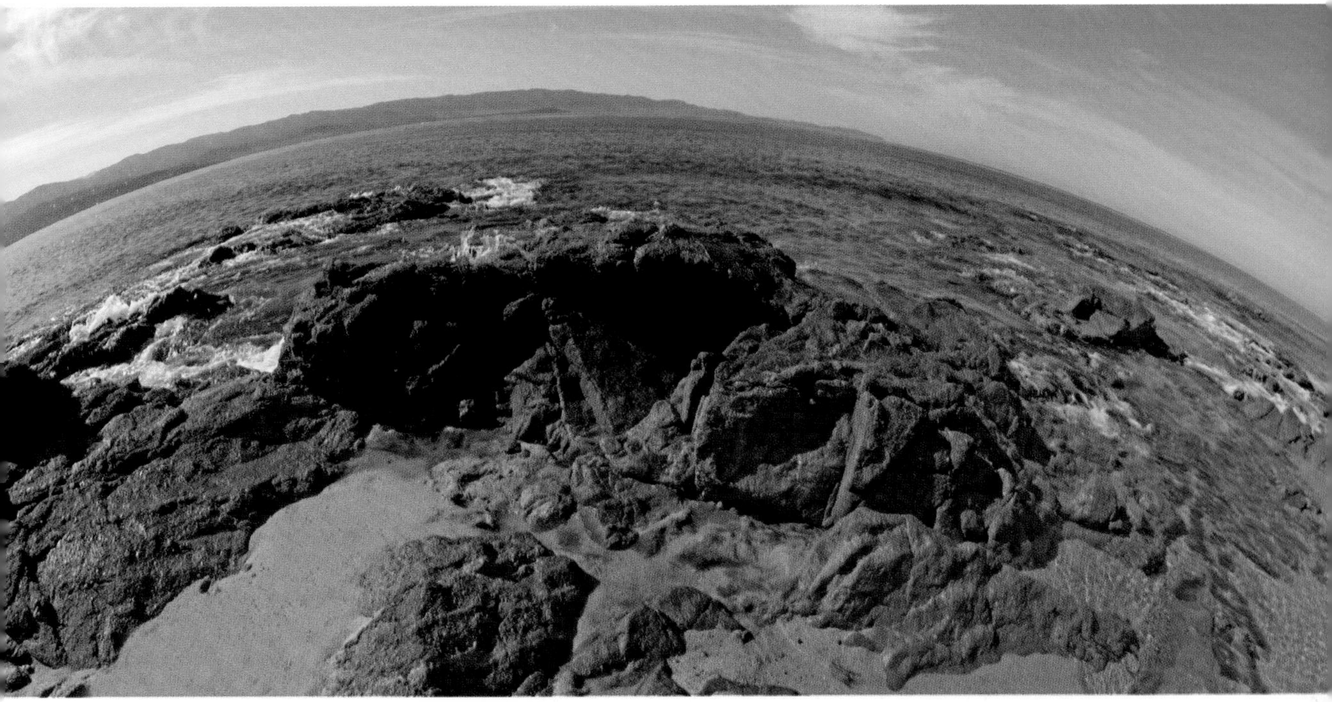

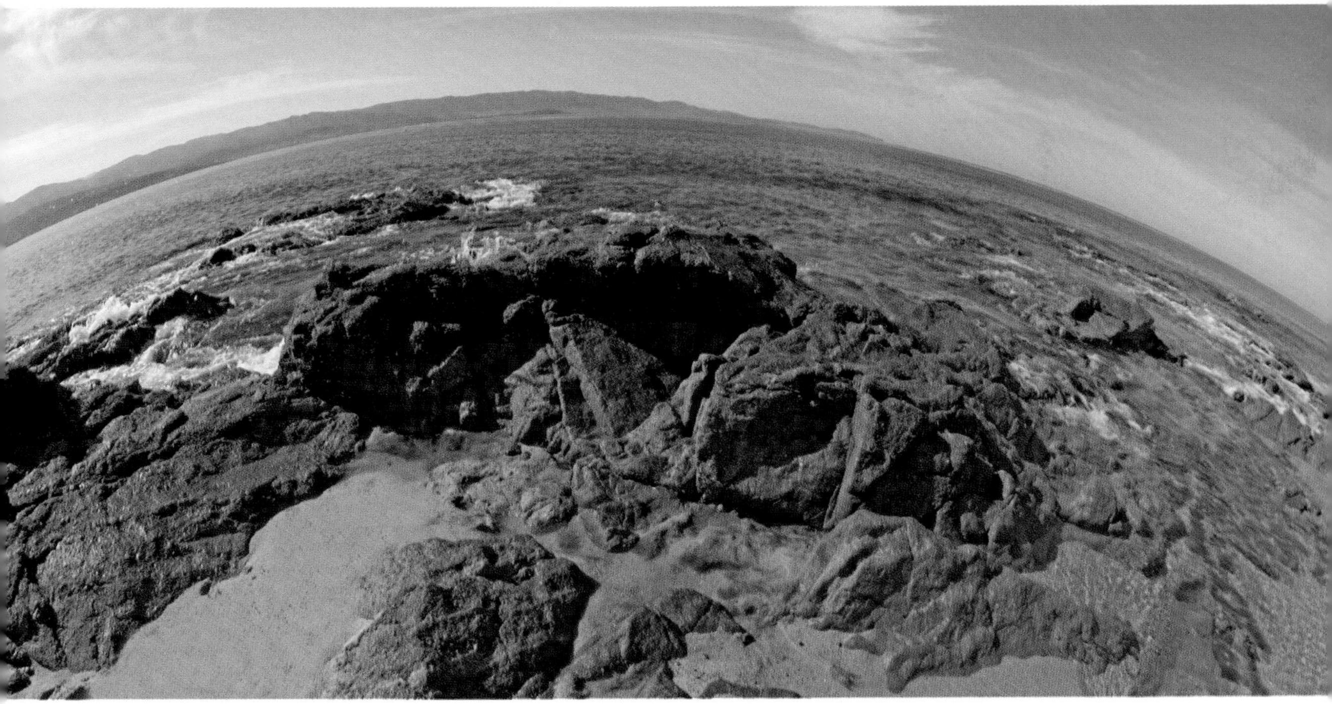

Adjustment Layers Are a Must!

In this book, I talk about using Curves, Levels, Hue/Saturation, and other image adjustments. To save time in the lessons, I don't always remind you that in each instance, you must apply the adjustment using an Adjustment Layer.

However, you should always use an Adjustment Layer, because doing so is a nondestructive technique for applying adjustments. If you make adjustments directly on an image file, you are—that's right—using a destructive editing technique. I don't know about you, but if I

▲ FIGURE 2.59

Tech info: Canon EOS 1D Mark II, Canon 100-400mm IS lens with Canon 1.4X converter @ 400mm. Exposure: 1/250 sec. @ f/8. ISO 400.

have a once-in-a-lifetime photograph, such as this sunset picture of an elephant that I took in Botswana (**Figure 2.59**), I want to maintain as much image data as possible.

What's more, when you save your file as a layered TIFF or Photoshop (PSD) file, you save all the Adjustment Layers. If you change your mind later about an adjustment you made, you can trash the Adjustment Layer and start over.

The easiest and fastest way to create an Adjustment Layer is to click the Adjustment Layer icon at the bottom of the Layers palette (**Figure 2.60**). Doing so opens the Adjustment Layer list. You can also create an Adjustment Layer by going to Layer > New Adjustment Layer. However, because your Layers palette will most likely be open when you're enhancing your images, it's faster to click the Adjustment Layer icon in that palette.

Click the type of Adjustment Layer you want, and a new Adjustment Layer is created above your image in the Layers palette (**Figure 2.61**). Your adjustments are made on that layer, not on your image. You can create multiple Adjustment Layers for additional creative enhancements.

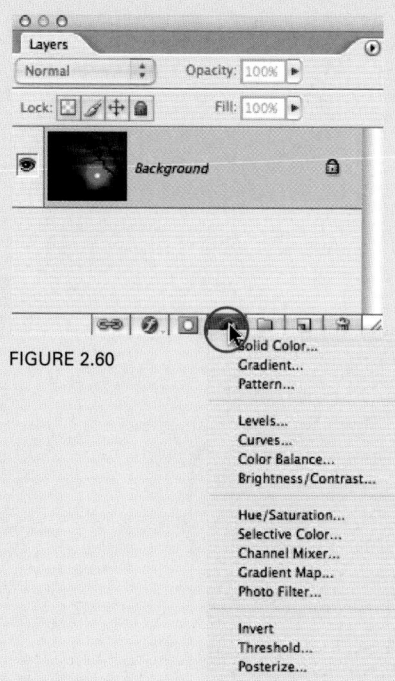

FIGURE 2.60

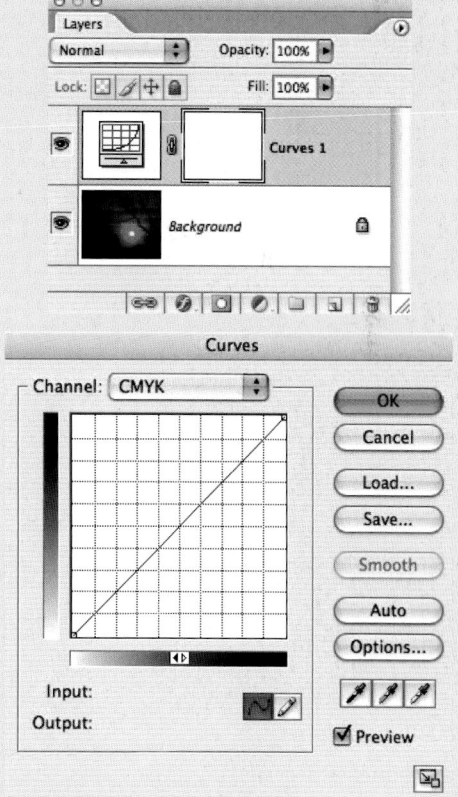

FIGURE 2.61

3 Creative-Image Artistry

CREATIVELY, YOU'RE AT THE MIDPOINT of this book. You've read about taking better pictures and applying some basic image adjustments to your images. If you've experimented with the techniques I suggested, you've gotten a glimpse of the power of seeing creatively when taking pictures and the power of Photoshop when working on your images in your digital darkroom.

Now it's time to dive a little deeper into the creative world of Photoshop. In this chapter, you'll learn how to create your own reality (with your images), which is totally cool. You'll see, among other things, how easy it is to change the time of day, control the weather, create an image that looks like it was taken before you were born, change one or all of the colors in a scene, put someone on the "Photoshop Diet," and, following our creative-image artistry theme, create the type of image that surrealist artist Salvador Dali might create if he were alive today and using a digital camera and Photoshop. Wallace Stevens wrote "Reality is the beginning not the end."

WHAT ARE YOU WAITING FOR? BEGIN!

All About Hue

Changing the hue affects the overall look of a color photograph. *Hue* is the actual color of an object. The hue of a red apple in a photograph is red. Other factors make that color, or any color, look different. For example, increasing the saturation of the picture gives the apple a deeper shade of red, and decreasing the saturation makes the apple look less vibrant. Increasing the brightness (using Levels, Curves, or Brightness) also makes the apple look less vibrant. Decreasing the brightness gives the photograph a deeper, richer look. Increasing the contrast can

▲ FIGURE 3.1

Tech info: Canon EOS 1D Mark II, Canon 50mm Macro lens. Exposure: 1/60 sec. @ f/16. ISO 100.

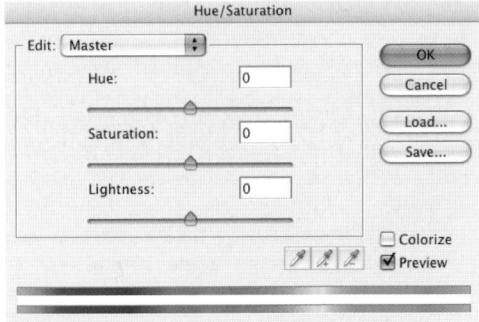

FIGURE 3.2

FIGURE 3.3

make the apple look crisper, whereas decreasing it makes it look less crisp. Hue works with saturation, brightness, and contrast—and you.

In this lesson, I use a still-life picture of tulips in a hand-painted vase to illustrate the possibilities of varying the hue (Figure 3.1).

In Photoshop, you can control hue by going to Image > Adjustments > Hue/Saturation (press Command-U: Mac or Ctrl-U: Win) and then adjusting the Hue slider (Figure 3.2). When you do that with the Edit: Master option selected, you change the hue of all the colors in an image. This is the result when I adjusted the Hue slider to –51 (with Edit: Master selected) (Figure 3.3). And here's what happened when I adjusted the Hue slider to +138 (again, with Edit: Master selected) (Figure 3.4).

But there's more to adjusting hue. You can adjust the individual colors (Reds, Yellows, Greens, Cyans, Blues, and Magentas) by clicking on the Edit drop-down menu and then scrolling to the specific color you want to adjust (Figure 3.5). For example, to adjust only the yellows in the tulip image, I selected Edit: Yellows and moved the slider to –51. Notice that the color of the flowers has changed from my original picture, but the background is still the same color (Figure 3.6).

FIGURE 3.4

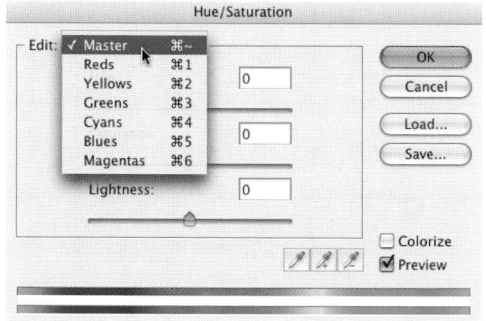

FIGURE 3.5

FIGURE 3.6

Speaking of the background in the flower image, changing it is also no problem. Here I selected Edit: Blues and adjusted the slider to –43 (Figure 3.7).

Moving the different sliders gives you virtually endless hue possibilities.

In the next image, I wanted to change the young woman's blue outfit to more of a blue/green. To do so, I selected Edit: Blues and adjusted the Hue slider to –68 (Figures 3.8 and 3.9).

For extra color enjoyment, play around with the Saturation and Lightness sliders in this dialog box, too!

FIGURE 3.7

▶ FIGURE 3.8

Tech info: Canon EOS 1D Mark II, Canon 70-200mm IS lens @ 200mm. Exposure: 1/125 sec. @ f/4.5. ISO 400.

FIGURE 3.9

▲ FIGURE 3.10

Tech info: Canon A2E,
28-105mm lens @ 105mm.
Exposure: 1/125 sec. @ f/8.
ISO 100.

Move the Clock Ahead

Photoshop gives you control over many aspects of your photographs. You even have the ability to make a photograph taken during the cool light of midday look as though it were taken during the late afternoon hours, when the light has a warmer and more pleasing quality.

There are several options for changing the time of day (so to speak) when a photograph was taken. Here are my favorites.

I took this photograph around midday from the top of the World Trade Center in New York City (**Figure 3.10**). As expected, the quality of the light was cool, giving the photograph a cool tint. The photograph also lacks contrast—something a setting sun increases in a scene by creating strong shadows. (Looking at this photograph stirs up mixed emotions for me. I included it in this book as a reminder of happier times.)

When you understand a challenge (fixing the cool color and low contrast, in this case), it's easy to figure out a solution in Photoshop. To warm up the photograph, I went to Image > Adjustments > Color Balance (press Command-B: Mac or Ctrl-B: Win) and, by adjusting the Red and Yellow sliders, boosted those tones in the photograph (**Figure 3.11**). To increase the contrast, I chose Image > Adjustment > Brightness/Contrast and boosted the Contrast slider (**Figure 3.12**). That doesn't create shadows, but it tricks the eye into thinking the picture was taken later in the day.

Here's the enhanced image, which has more vibrant colors and contrast than my original (**Figure 3.13**).

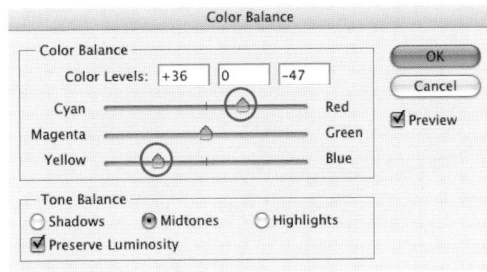

FIGURE 3.11

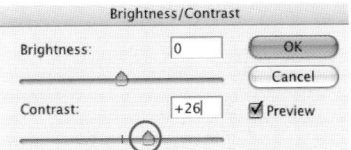

FIGURE 3.12

▼ FIGURE 3.13

▲ FIGURE 3.14

Tech info: Canon EOS 1D Mark II, Canon 100-400mm IS lens @ 300mm. Exposure: 1/125 sec. @ f/5.6. ISO 400.

FIGURE 3.15

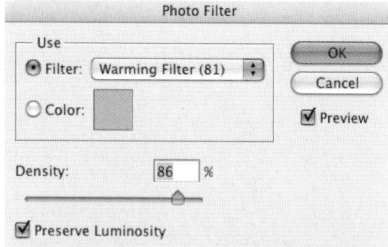

Let's look at another technique for moving the clock ahead. This time, I'll use a picture I took at Jungle World at the Bronx Zoo (Figure 3.14).

In the earlier example, boosting the red and yellow tones warmed the picture. You can also warm up a picture by using the Warming filter (Image > Adjustments > Photo Filter), which brings up the Photo Filter dialog box (Figure 3.15). Move the Density slider until the picture is warmed to your liking. Here's the result of using Photoshop's Warming filter on my photograph (Figure 3.16).

Here's a picture I took on a beach in Corsica (Figure 3.17). Again, I wanted to simulate the effect of the picture being taken late in the day. Understanding what was wrong with the picture (low saturation as well as the aforementioned characteristics) helped me find a solution.

To increase the saturation, I went to Image > Adjustments > Hue/Saturation and boosted the Saturation slider (Figure 3.18). Then, to see into the shadows, I chose Image > Adjustments > Shadow/Highlight and boosted the Shadows slider (Figure 3.19).

As a final touch, I did a bit of cropping; the result was a picture with more impact (Figure 3.20).

FIGURE 3.16

▲ FIGURE 3.17

Tech info: Canon EOS 1Ds Mark II, Canon 16-35mm lens @ 16mm. Exposure: 1/125 sec. @ f/16. ISO 100.

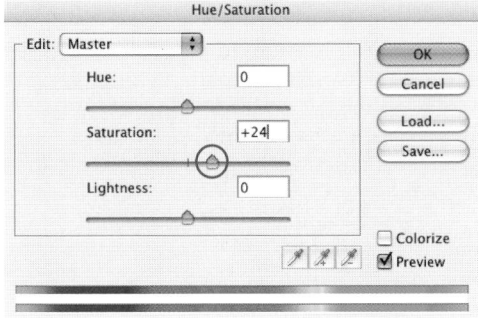

FIGURE 3.18

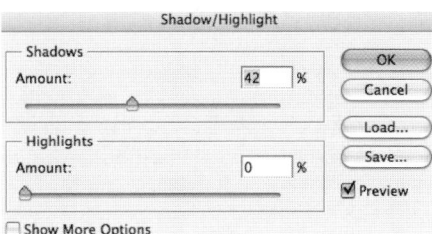

FIGURE 3.19

FIGURE 3.20

After Midnight

In the previous lesson, you learned how to turn the clock ahead by warming up a picture. Now, I'll show you how to transform a picture taken during daylight hours into one that looks as though it were taken at midnight—on a night when the full moon was shining brightly.

First, think about how a picture taken by moonlight differs in light quality from a picture taken at noon. The nighttime picture is cooler, has less saturated colors, and looks softer than a daytime picture. Knowing that, you can make the appropriate enhancements in Photoshop.

Here's a picture I took of a jaguar in the Belize Zoo (**Figure 3.21**). To cool off the picture, I went to Image > Adjustments > Color Balance (Command-B: Mac or Ctrl-B: Win) and used the sliders to boost the Blue and Cyan tones (**Figure 3.22**). Next, I chose Image > Adjustments > Hue/Saturation and used the Saturation slider to slightly desaturate the

▼ FIGURE 3.21

Tech info: Canon EOS 1v, Canon 28-105mm lens @ 105mm. Exposure: 1/250 sec. @ f/8. ISO 400.

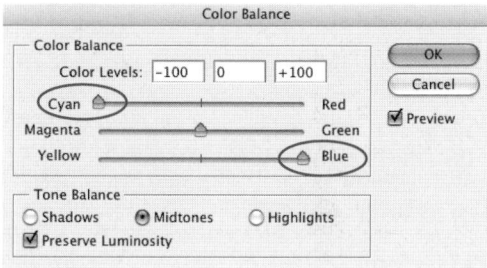

FIGURE 3.22

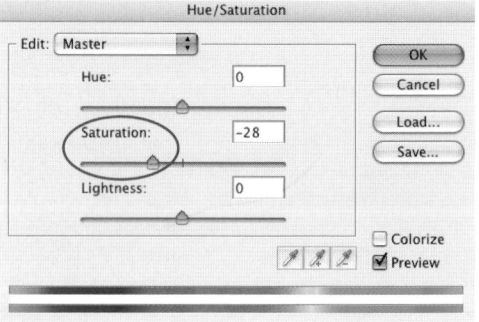

FIGURE 3.23

image (Figure 3.23). To soften the picture, I went to Filter > Blur > Gaussian Blur and added just a touch of blur (Figure 3.24).

The resulting picture is cooler, less saturated, and softer—with one more added touch (Figure 3.25). I used the Burn tool (press O: Mac or Win) to slightly darken the area around the jaguar to create the impression that the big cat was standing in a beam of moonlight and the surrounding area was in a shadow.

FIGURE 3.24

FIGURE 3.25

By the Light of the Moon

There are other ways to create a midnight effect. One is to use the Midnight Sepia filter (also available in Blue, Green, and Violet versions) that's found in Nik Software, Inc.'s Photoshop-compatible plug-in Nik Color Efex Pro 2.0. (www.niksoftware.com). Let's look at what this filter can do.

When you open the Midnight Sepia filter, you get a dialog box with controls for Blur, Contrast, Brightness, and Color (**Figure 3.26**). You can select a custom effect.

My picture looks like an evening shot immediately after applying the Midnight Sepia filter (**Figure 3.27**). It looks OK; but as always, and I mean always, I play around with other adjustments to see how a picture can be enhanced—because I feel that in Photoshop, a photograph is never finished. I went to Fade > Edit and faded the filter to 62% (**Figure 3.28**). Then, I chose Image > Adjust > Color Balance and increased the Cyan and Blue tones in the picture (**Figure 3.29**).

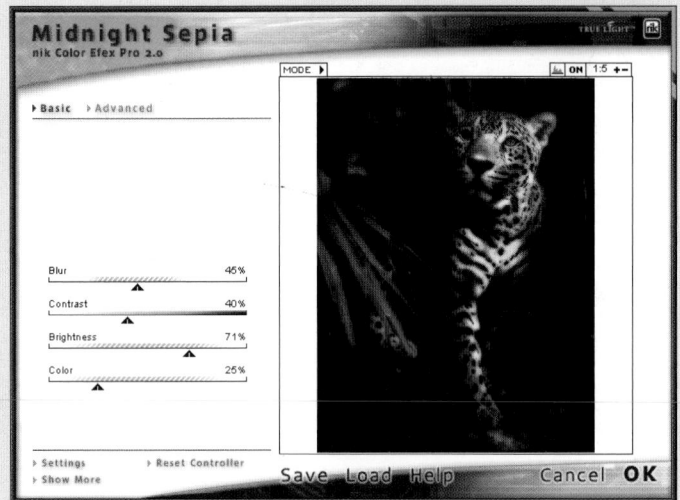

FIGURE 3.26

FIGURE 3.27

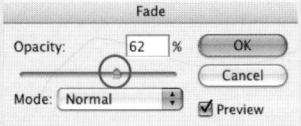

FIGURE 3.28

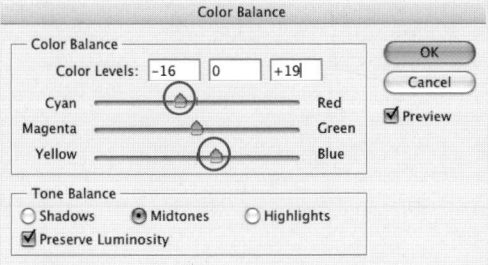

FIGURE 3.29

The final image creates the impression that the jaguar was photographed at midnight on a moonlit night (**Figure 3.30**).

Here's another example of how Nik's Midnight filter can make a straight shot look a bit more creative by softening and darkening it (**Figure 3.31**).

FIGURE 3.30

▲ FIGURE 3.31

Tech info: Canon EOS 1v, Canon 70-200mm lens @ 200mm. Exposure: 1/125 sec. @ f/2.8. ISO 100.

▲ FIGURE 3.32

Tech info: Canon EOS 1v, Canon 28-105mm lens @ 105mm. Exposure: 1/125 sec. @ f/8. ISO 64.

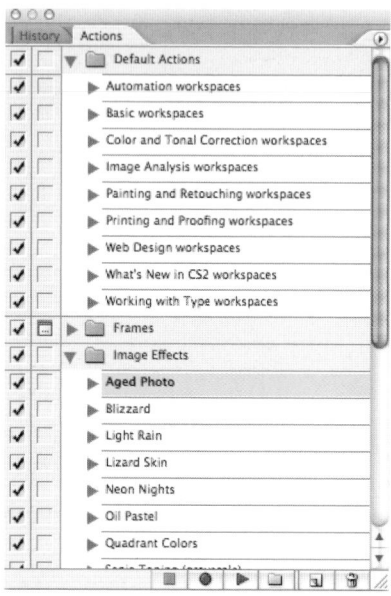

FIGURE 3.33

Speed-Aging a Photograph

One of the creative effects I like to apply to certain images is to age the photograph. I say "certain images" because the image must lend itself to looking old, like the images I've included in this lesson. Why do I like the effect? Well, first off, when we remove the sharpness and true color from an image, we remove some of the reality. When we remove some of the reality, an image often looks more creative. Secondly, I just think the effect looks cool!

Photoshop offers a built-in Action (an automatic instruction found under Window > Actions) that makes the process fast and easy—and fun.

I'll begin with a picture of a man I took in Hong Kong (**Figure 3.32**). He's asking me for a dollar. I had already paid him a dollar to take his picture and was about to take another. The bucks were well worth it.

After I clicked the Aged Photo Action in the Actions palette (**Figure 3.33**), my image looked like a faded photograph that was taken decades ago (**Figure 3.34**).

TIP: If you don't see the Aged Photo Action in the list, you need to load the Image Effects group of Actions by clicking the little fly-out arrow at the top right of the Actions palette and then scrolling down to Image Effects in the pop-up window.

You can also age a photograph by applying the Sepia Toning Action. On the next page, you'll see a picture I took of a cowboy in Texas look as though it was taken way before digital cameras were invented (**Figures 3.35** and **3.36**).

After you apply one Action, you can continue to apply other Actions to your images. To make my Great Wall of China picture look as though it was taken on a rainy day shortly after the completion of this wonder of the world, I applied both the Aged Photo Action and the Light Rain Action (**Figures 3.37** and **3.38**).

OK, it's your turn to take action!

FIGURE 3.34

▲ FIGURES 3.35 and 3.36

Tech info: Canon EOS D30, Canon
28-135mm lens @ 100mm. Exposure: 1/125
sec. @ f/5.6. ISO 200.

◀ FIGURES 3.37 and 3.38 ▼

Tech info: Canon EOS D30, Canon 24mm
lens. Exposure: 1/125 sec. @ f/11. ISO 100.

Control the Weather

In Photoshop, you can play Mother Nature, to a degree—by adding rain or snow to a picture. You can easily do so by using Photoshop's Light Rain and Blizzard Actions. However, there is more to the forecast, so to speak. Let's take a look.

My goal was to make this picture of a horse and rider taken on a sunny day look as though it was taken on a rainy afternoon (**Figure 3.39**). Before adding the rain, I needed to do some work on the photo, which has strong colors due to the bright sunlight.

▼ FIGURE 3.39

Tech info: Canon EOS 1D Mark II, Canon 70-200mm lens @ 200mm. Exposure: 1/500 sec. @ f/8. ISO 400.

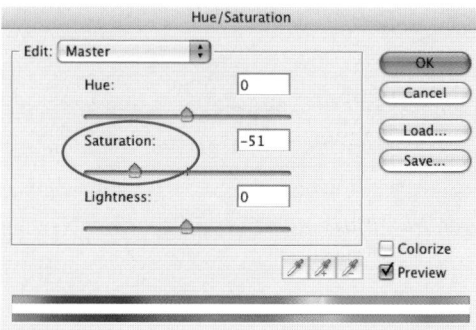

FIGURE 3.40

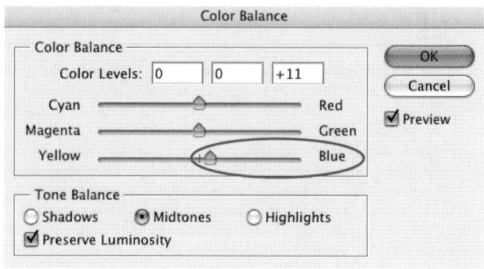

FIGURE 3.41

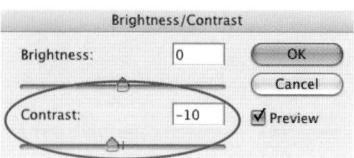

FIGURE 3.42

My first step was to go to Image > Adjustments > Hue/Saturation and use the Saturation slider to desaturate the image (**Figure 3.40**). A setting of –51 did it.

Pictures taken in the rain have cooler tones than pictures taken on sunny days. So, my next step was to choose Image > Adjustments > Color Balance and boost Blue by +11 (**Figure 3.41**).

Rainy-day pictures also have less contrast than sunny-day pictures. I went to Image > Adjustments > Brightness/Contrast and reduced the Contrast by –10 (**Figure 3.42**).

It was time to add the rain. To do so, I applied the Light Rain Action (**Figure 3.43**).

Whoa, partner! Now it looks like the rider is galloping through a light rain (**Figure 3.44**). I achieved my goal.

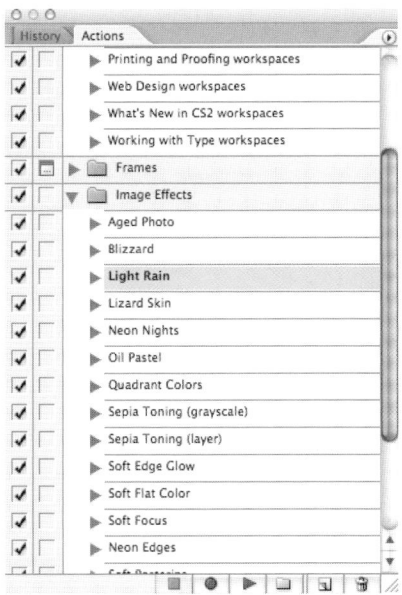

FIGURE 3.43

FIGURE 3.44

Filter Transformation

Creating more artistic pictures using Photoshop's built-in filters, as well as Photoshop-compatible plug-in filters, is fun and easy to do.

This lesson looks briefly at just a few of the millions (literally) of creative possibilities. In the next lesson, you'll see how to take more creative control over the filters.

▼ FIGURE 3.45

Tech info: Canon EOS 1D Mark II, Canon 16-35mm lens @ 16mm. Exposure: 1/125 sec. @ f/8. ISO 100.

As an example, I'll use a picture I took of a lifeguard stand in Miami's South Beach (**Figure 3.45**).

One of my favorite creative filters is the Graphic Pen filter (Filter > Sketch > Graphic Pen). You can access this as well as all of Photoshop's other filters through the Filter Gallery (Filter > Filter Gallery). When you select this filter, you get a dialog box that offers several creative choices (**Figure 3.46**). You can control the Stroke Length, Light/Dark Balance, and Stroke Direction; play around with these sliders for customized effects. After you're pleased with the image in the Preview window, click OK to apply the filter to the image.

TIP: If a few of the options in the Filter menu are grayed out and unavailable, you may first need to duplicate the background layer and add a layer mask to the duplicate layer.

When I applied the Graphic Pen filter to my picture, it looked like a painter's sketch (**Figure 3.47**). But this wasn't the end of the creative process—it was only the beginning.

I softened the filter's intensity (opacity) by going to Edit > Fade and moving the slider to the left (**Figure 3.48**).

That's more like it. I faded the filter so some of the color of my original photograph was still visible (**Figure 3.49**).

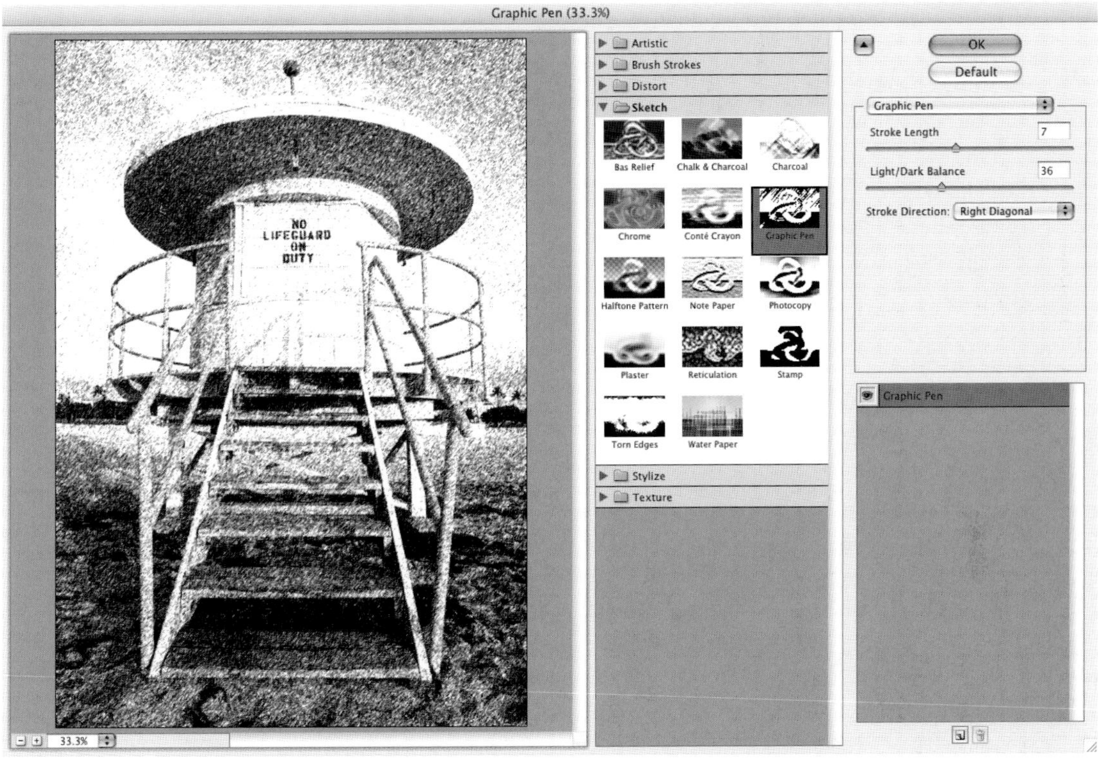

Graphic Pen (33.3%)

FIGURE 3.46

FIGURE 3.47

FIGURE 3.48

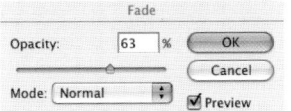

FIGURE 3.49

chapter three *Creative-Image Artistry* **77**

One of the cool things I like to do with the Graphic Pen filter is to change the color of the "pen" I use. I clicked the Foreground Color box at the bottom of the Tool Bar to open the Color Picker dialog box. Then, I clicked a color in the Color Picker, and the foreground color changed to my selected color (a light blue, in this case) (**Figure 3.50**).

FIGURE 3.50

Compare the effect of using the blue pen in this example to that of the black pen in the previous example (in which black was set as the foreground color) (**Figure 3.51**).

Here are three more examples of Photoshop filters, all using the default settings:

♦ Dry Brush (Filter > Artistic > Dry Brush) (**Figure 3.52**)

♦ Rough Pastels (Filter > Artistic > Rough Pastels) (**Figure 3.53**)

♦ Ink Outlines (Filters > Brush Strokes > Ink Outlines) (**Figure 3.54**)

Filters and plug-in filters open up a new world of creative options. Play around with the filters and their sliders, fading the filter and changing the foreground color (you can't do this with all filters). You'll be pleasantly surprised when you get an unexpected effect. Just don't overdo it—too much of a good thing (applying the same filter to many photos) can get boring.

FIGURE 3.51

FIGURE 3.52

FIGURE 3.53

FIGURE 3.54

More Possibilities with Plug-ins

Photoshop-compatible plug-ins expand your creative horizons. One of my favorites is Nik Color Efex Pro from Nik Software. Here are two of the dozens of effects in this way-cool filter set:

◆ Color Stylizer (**Figure 3.55**)
◆ Duplex Monochrome (**Figure 3.56**)

FIGURE 3.55

FIGURE 3.56

A Note Paper Effect

Photoshop's filters have a creative mind of their own. They make creative decisions for you, if you go with the default settings, as you saw in the previous lesson. However, you can change Photoshop's mind and persuade it to think more like you do.

Let's begin with a straight shot I took of a banded peacock butterfly, to which I'll apply the Note Paper filter (Filter > Sketch > Note Paper) (**Figure 3.57**).

Filters are located in the Filter menu or, as I mentioned in the previous section, through the Filter Gallery (Filter > Filter Gallery). When you apply a

filter, you get a dialog box with a window that shows the effects of the default settings for that filter. By moving the sliders (Image Balance, Graininess, and Relief, in the case of the Note Paper filter), you can fine-tune the effect to suit your own creative vision. The picture window showed me Photoshop's creative vision for how the Note Paper filter should be applied to my butterfly picture (**Figure 3.58**).

After you click OK, the filter is applied to the image. Here's a better look at how the Note Paper filter looked when I applied it to my image (**Figure 3.59**).

NOTE: Keep in mind that the larger the file, the longer it will take for the filter to be applied.

▲ FIGURE 3.57

Tech info: Canon EOS 1D, Canon 50mm Macro lens, Canon Macro Ring Lite MR-14EX. Exposure: 1/60 sec. @ f/22. ISO 100.

TIP: Some filters aren't available for use with CMYK and/or 16-bit files; to apply filters for those types of images, you must change the mode (Image > Mode) to RGB Color and/or 8 Bits/Channel.

As I mentioned, you can adjust a filter's sliders to fine-tune your image, using Photoshop's imagination. But you can also change Photoshop's thinking by applying one or more adjustments—including Levels, Curves, Hue/Saturation, Color Balance, and so on—to an image.

I like to do something else immediately after applying a filter: fading that filter. I went to Edit > Fade (the filter's name appears after the word *Fade*) and moved the slider to change the Opacity (intensity) of the filter. While in Normal mode, I reduced the Opacity to 50 percent (**Figure 3.60**).

FIGURE 3.58

FIGURE 3.59

FIGURE 3.60

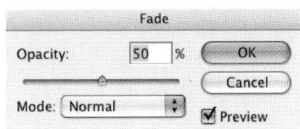

FIGURE 3.61

Here's the result of reducing the Note Paper filter's Opacity by 50 percent—and increasing the Contrast (Image > Adjustments > Contrast) by 40 percent (**Figure 3.61**). I like this effect much better than the default.

You can make even more suggestions to the creative mind of Photoshop. By clicking the Foreground Color box at the bottom of the Tool Bar and then clicking a color in the Color Picker, you can change the foreground color—which in turn can affect the color of the filter. (I say "can affect" because not all filters are influenced by the foreground color.) In this case, I picked a red color (**Figure 3.62**).

FIGURE 3.63

Changing the foreground color to red totally changed the Note Paper filter's default effect (**Figure 3.63**).

Fading the Note Paper filter with the red foreground created one of a gazillion other creative filter effects that are available in Photoshop (**Figure 3.64**).

Finally, I picked a dark blue as the foreground color, applied the Note Paper filter, and then faded that filter. The variations are endless (**Figure 3.65**).

When it comes to applying a filter to one of your images, remember that you can always change your mind—and Photoshop's!

FIGURE 3.64

FIGURE 3.62

FIGURE 3.65

Create a Pinhole Camera Effect

▼ FIGURE 3.66

Tech info: Canon EOS 1Ds Mark II, Canon 16-35mm lens @ 20mm. Exposure: 1/125 sec. @ f/16. ISO 100.

As a professional travel photographer, I need to shoot with a top-of-the-line digital SLR camera. The images from my camera are super sharp. What's more, due to the camera's sensor and image processor, I get relatively little noise (what we used to call *grain* in film) in my pictures.

I love the detail-packed raw files that my camera delivers. However, I thought it would be fun to try to simulate the effect of the most basic and affordable camera—a pinhole camera (a camera with no true lens or shutter, which you can make out of an oatmeal container)—on one of my images. Pictures from pinhole cameras look soft and grainy, due to the pinhole "lens" and the fast film that is needed to record the image. The pictures also have dark edges, due to the light falloff passing through the small hole.

I like the pinhole camera effect! Here's how I created it.

I'll use a picture I took of an old homestead in Oregon (**Figure 3.66**).

Adding film grain to my photo was easy. I went to Filter > Artistic > Film Grain and played around with the sliders to get the desired effect (more or less grain) (**Figure 3.67**). Applying the Film Grain filter removed some of the scene's reality, creating a more artistic image (**Figure 3.68**). However, I wasn't finished. The next step was to remove some of the color (more of the reality) from the scene. I did that by choosing Image > Adjustments > Hue/Saturation and moving the Saturation slider to the left until I got the desired result (**Figure 3.69**). The image was getting close to the effect I envisioned (**Figure 3.70**).

![Film Grain dialog box showing Artistic filter options including Colored Pencil, Cutout, Dry Brush, Film Grain, Fresco, Neon Glow, Paint Daubs, Palette Knife, Plastic Wrap, Poster Edges, Rough Pastels, Smudge Stick, Sponge, Underpainting, Watercolor. Film Grain settings: Grain 12, Highlight Area 1, Intensity 1. Image of an old weathered building in a field.]

FIGURE 3.67

FIGURE 3.68

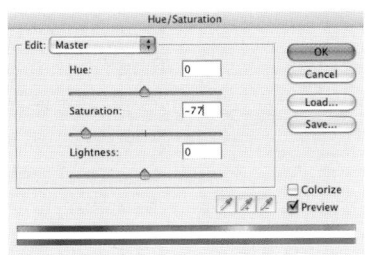

FIGURE 3.69

FIGURE 3.70

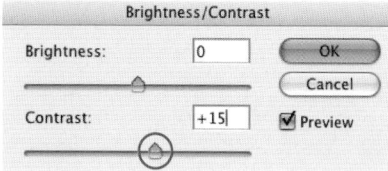

FIGURE 3.71

The image looked a bit flat to me. So, I went to Image > Adjustments > Brightness/Contrast and boosted the Contrast a bit (**Figure 3.71**). I could also have used Curves (press M: Mac or Win) or Levels (press L: Mac or Win) to make a contrast adjustment to the picture.

In "Draw Attention to a Subject" in Chapter 2, I discussed the technique for darkening the edges of an image. By applying it to this image, I simulated the darker edges I'd get in a picture taken with a pinhole camera (**Figure 3.72**).

Pinhole cameras are mostly used for landscapes. But you can have fun applying the digital pinhole camera effect to portraits, too.

Here's how the effect transformed a picture I took of a little girl in a remote Embera village in Panama into a more artistic image (**Figures 3.73** and **3.74**).

If you want the best quality digital file, get a top-of-the-line digital SLR. For the cleanest picture, shoot at the lowest ISO setting. But keep in mind that sometimes a grainy, soft picture may look more artistic than a technically perfect photograph.

FIGURE 3.72

▶ FIGURES 3.73 and 3.74

Tech info: Canon EOS 1Ds Mark II, Canon 70-200mm lens @ 200mm. Exposure: 1/125 sec. @ f/5.6. ISO 400.

▲ FIGURE 3.75

Tech info: Canon EOS 1Ds Mark II, Canon 16-35mm lens @ 16mm. Exposure: 1/125 sec. @ f/11. ISO 100.

Create a Basic Montage

Creating a *montage* (a composite of two or more images) is a great way to express your creativity. This lesson looks at some basic montage techniques. I'll discuss more advanced montage techniques in "Create an Artistic Montage" in Chapter 4.

I'll make the first basic montage using two pictures I took in Botswana (**Figures 3.75** and **3.76**). My idea for this montage was to create an image that conveyed the spirit of Botswana—with a faint image of the leopard in the sky.

With both images open, I dragged my picture of the leopard onto my sunset picture. Now I had a two-layer document, with the leopard on the top layer (**Figure 3.77**).

To create only a faint vision of the leopard in the sky, I opened the Layers palette (Window > Layers) and reduced the Opacity to 36% (**Figure 3.78**).

Now it was time to erase the area around the leopard. I selected the Eraser tool (press E: Mac or Win) and chose a medium-size brush. For more control over my erasing, I went to the Menu Bar and reduced the Opacity to 39% (**Figure 3.79**). Reducing the Opacity makes the erasing process happen at a slower rate.

◀ FIGURE 3.76

Tech info: Canon EOS
1Ds Mark II, Canon 100-
400mm IS lens w/1.4X tele
converter. Exposure: 1/250
sec. @ f/8. ISO 400.

FIGURE 3.77

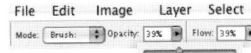

FIGURE 3.78

FIGURE 3.79

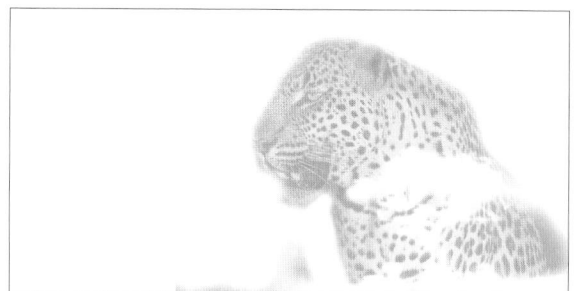

FIGURE 3.80

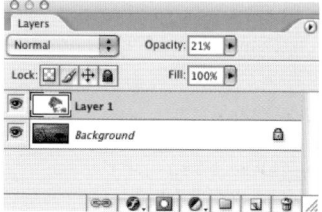

FIGURE 3.81

To check whether I was doing a good job erasing the desired area, I turned off the bottom layer in the Layers palette (by clicking the eye icon). Here you can see that I haven't done the greatest job so far (**Figure 3.80**). Good thing I checked; more erasing was needed. To make the image of the leopard more subdued, I reduced the opacity of the top layer to 21% (**Figure 3.81**). Here's my final "Spirit of Botswana" montage (**Figure 3.82**).

That's about as basic as it gets when it comes to making a montage. Let's look at a few more important steps in montage creation.

Here's another picture I took in Botswana, and a picture I took in another wild place: Miami's South Beach (**Figures 3.83** and **3.84**).

FIGURE 3.82

▲ FIGURE 3.83

Tech info: Canon EOS 1Ds Mark II, Canon
16-35mm lens @ 20mm. Exposure: 1/60 sec.
@ f/4. ISO 200.

▲ FIGURE 3.84

Tech info: Canon EOS 1D
Mark II, Canon 28-135mm
IS lens @ 100mm. Studio
strobes. Exposure: 1/60 sec.
@ f/8. ISO 100.

FIGURE 3.85

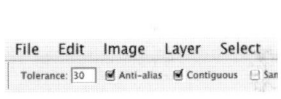

FIGURE 3.86

Following the same technique of opening the two images and dragging
one on top of the other, my new document looked like this (**Figure 3.85**).
Again, I wanted to eliminate the background. I could have used the Eraser
tool, but a quicker method is available when the background is plain:
using the Magic Wand tool (press W: Mac or Win). The Magic Wand tool
selects areas of an image based on color, when you click that color.

This tool requires you to make some important choices. First, you need to
set the Tolerance on the Menu Bar (**Figure 3.86**). Set too low a Tolerance,
and only areas with small variations in color (from your original color) will
be selected. Set too high a Tolerance, and you'll select areas with large
variations in color. For my model image, I set the Tolerance to 30.

FIGURE 3.87

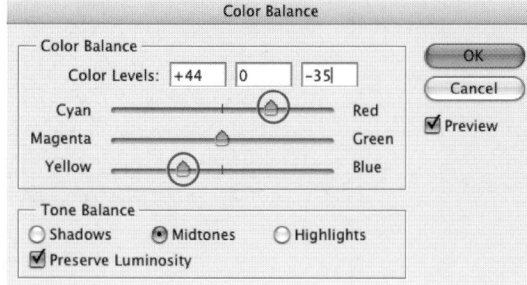

FIGURE 3.88

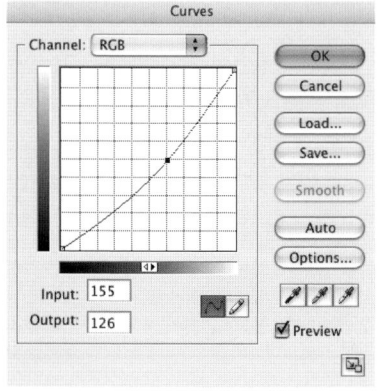

FIGURE 3.89

Anti-Alias is another choice. For a smoother transition between the selected and unselected areas, I chose Anti-Alias.

Next, you must decide whether to check or uncheck Contiguous. Checking it picks only the selected colors that are connected—in this case, between the model's arm and her body. Choosing not to check it selects all the similar colors in the image. I chose Contiguous for more control.

After all that work, my montage looked like this (**Figure 3.87**). What's wrong? The color temperature of the light doesn't match in the two pictures. The sunset picture is very warm, and the model shot is cool. Plus, the model image is brighter than the sunset image. Here's how I fixed the color.

TIP: For a smoother look between the two images, use the Eraser tool, and trace the outline of the inserted subject. That technique makes your montage look more natural.

To warm up the image, I went to Image > Adjustment > Color Balance (press Command-B: Mac or Ctrl-B: Win) and increased the Red and Yellow tones in the image (**Figure 3.88**). Then, I chose Image > Adjustment > Curves and pulled down the Curve line (**Figure 3.89**).

That's more like it! The color and brightness values of both images match, yielding a natural-looking montage (**Figure 3.90**).

I can't overstress the importance of trying to match the colors of the different images in a montage. Here's another example of how a matched-colored montage looks more realistic than a montage in which the colors of the different images don't match (**Figures 3.91** and **3.92**). Sure, the montage with the white seagull shows the true color of the bird; but when placed in a sunset scene, the white features take on a warmer cast (deeper shades of red and yellow).

FIGURE 3.90

▲ FIGURES 3.91 and 3.92 ▶

Tech info (for both figures): Canon EOS 1D Mark II, Canon 100-400mm IS lens @ 400mm. Exposure: 1/500 sec. @ f/5.6. ISO 200.

Liquify Reality

Salvador Dali, the 20th century's best-known surrealist artist, is famous for his painting of melting clocks. Those melting clocks were the inspiration for this lesson. As you'll see, you can use the Liquify filter (Filter > Liquify) to melt objects in a photograph for a surrealistic look.

Before I turn up the heat and start the melting, however, I'd like to share with you a more practical use of the Liquify filter: making a subject in a picture look thinner and more fit. Some folks call the following technique the "Photoshop Diet," which usually gets a few laughs at Photoshop World (a bi-annual gathering of Photoshop pros and fans). In reality, however, it's a practical effect that fashion photography retouchers use to make even top models look better.

▲ FIGURE 3.93

Tech info: Canon EOS D30, Canon 70-200mm lens @ 100mm. Exposure: 1/250 sec. @ f/5.6. ISO 200.

To illustrate the technique, I'll use a picture I took of a young woman in Cuba, who didn't need to go on a diet (**Figure 3.93**).

When you select the Liquify filter (press Shift-Command-X: Mac or Shift-Ctrl-X: Win), you get the Liquify dialog box, which includes a Preview window and Liquify tools and controls (**Figure 3.94**). At the upper left of the Tool Bar is the Forward Warp tool, which is the default. This tool lets you liquify pixels—melting them, twirling them, bending them, and stretching them. In this screenshot, I've circled the brush I used to reduce the woman's waistline; I did this by clicking her waistline, holding down my right mouse button, and moving the brush inward.

Here's the effect of applying the Photoshop Diet to the woman's waist, arms, legs, and neck (**Figure 3.95**).

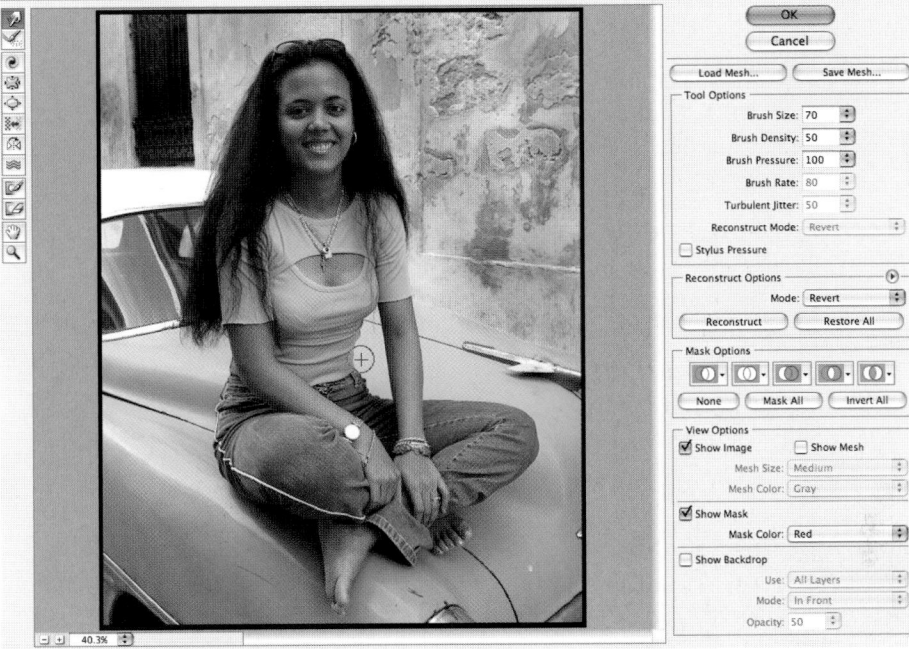

FIGURE 3.94

FIGURE 3.95

FIGURE 3.95

OK, let's get to the melting effect.

I'll use a picture of a flower I took in my backyard (**Figure 3.96**). In the Liquify dialog box, I moved the Forward Warp tool in a circular motion around the flower and then in a back-and-forth motion on the flower's stem (**Figure 3.97**). Here you can see the result of those quick mouse movements (**Figure 3.98**).

Talk about melting! In the next example, I used the Liquify filter to melt a hotel sign in Miami's South Beach, which is "hot, hot, hot" even in the winter due to the wild nightlife (**Figures 3.99** and **3.100**).

◀ FIGURE 3.96

Tech info: Canon EOS 1D, Canon 50mm Macro lens, Canon Macro Ring Lite MR-14EX. Exposure: 1/60 sec. @ f/22. ISO 100.

FIGURE 3.97

FIGURE 3.98

◀ FIGURES 3.99 and 3.100 ▼

Tech info: Canon EOS 1D, Canon 16-35mm lens @ 20mm. Exposure: 1/125 sec. @ f/8. ISO 400.

▲ FIGURE 3.101

Tech info: Canon EOS 1v, Canon 70-200mm zoom @ 200mm. Exposure: 1/250 sec. @ f/11. ISO 100.

Reflecting on an Image

"It's all done with mirrors" is a popular saying among professional magicians. These days, digital photography artists are using mirrors, of sorts, to create magical effects on their computer monitors. In a mirror image, one side of a frame is perfectly mirrored (reflected) on the opposite side of the frame—side to side or top to bottom. Here's how to do it.

Start with a visually strong picture. Actually, you have to start with a vision—an idea of how a subject will look when mirrored, or reflected, against itself. For this lesson, I'll use a picture I took in the desert of Rajasthan, India (**Figure 3.101**).

My first step was to select the entire image. I chose Select > All (press Command-A: Mac or Ctrl-A: Win) and then Edit > Copy (press Command-C: Mac or Ctrl-C: Win). That placed the image in my computer's memory.

Next, I chose File > New (press Command-N: Mac or Ctrl-N: Win) and clicked OK. A new, empty file exactly the same size as the original image was created. (Your image may look larger or smaller due to the percentage at which you're viewing your original picture. The viewing percentage is shown at the bottom left of the document window.) I chose Edit > Paste (press Command-V: Mac or Ctrl-V: Win) to paste my original picture into the new document (**Figure 3.102**).

While working with the newly created document, I went to Image > Rotate Canvas > Flip Vertically to create the reflection portion of what would be my final image (**Figure 3.103**).

FIGURE 3.102

FIGURE 3.103

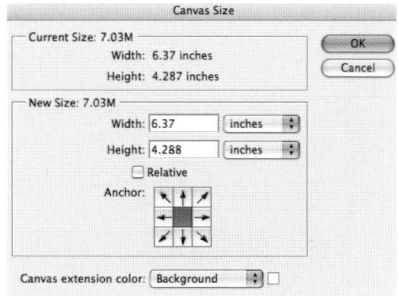

FIGURE 3.104

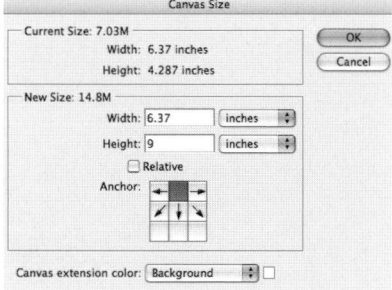

FIGURE 3.105

I went back to my original image and chose Image > Canvas Size to open the Canvas Size dialog box. To create the reflection, I doubled the height of the Canvas; to make things easy, I rounded up the height from 4.288 inches to 9 inches (**Figures 3.104** and **3.105**). Here you can see that the Canvas size is a little more than doubled in height (**Figure 3.106**).

I made sure I was viewing both images at the same magnification percentage. I clicked the upside-down image and dragged it into the newly created white space in the original image until the images were aligned (**Figure 3.107**). Next, I used the Crop tool (press C: Mac or Win) to crop out the white space at the bottom of the image (**Figure 3.108**). The upside-down image was on its own layer (**Figure 3.109**). That made the next step easy. With the top layer (the upside-down image) activated (shown in blue here and activated by clicking it), I went to Filter > Distort > Ocean Ripple (**Figure 3.110**) and played around with the Ripple Size and Ripple Magnitude sliders until I was pleased with the result.

FIGURE 3.106

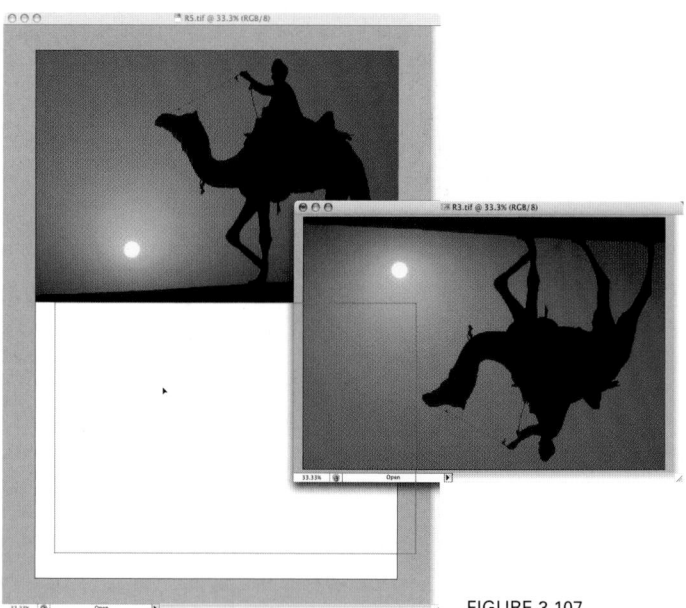

FIGURE 3.107

FIGURE 3.108

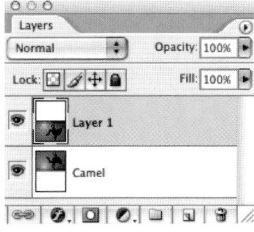

FIGURE 3.109

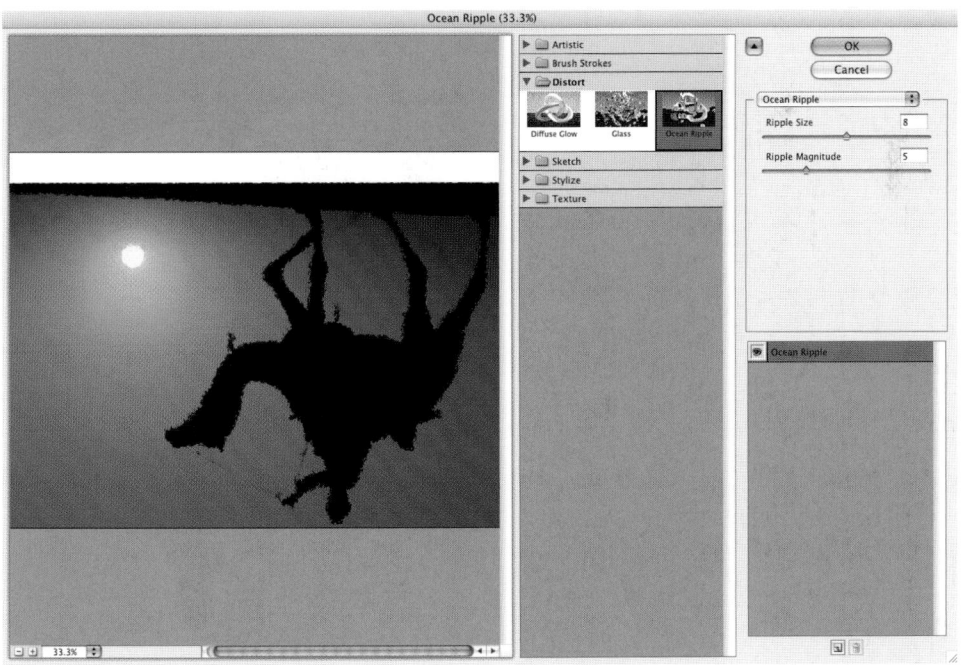

FIGURE 3.110

Here's the final image—a perfect reflection (**Figure 3.111**).

Of course, you need to work with an original picture that will make a nice reflection image. On the next page are two more examples that use the reflection technique—one a tightly cropped vertical shot and one created horizontally (**Figures 3.112** and **3.113**).

FIGURE 3.111

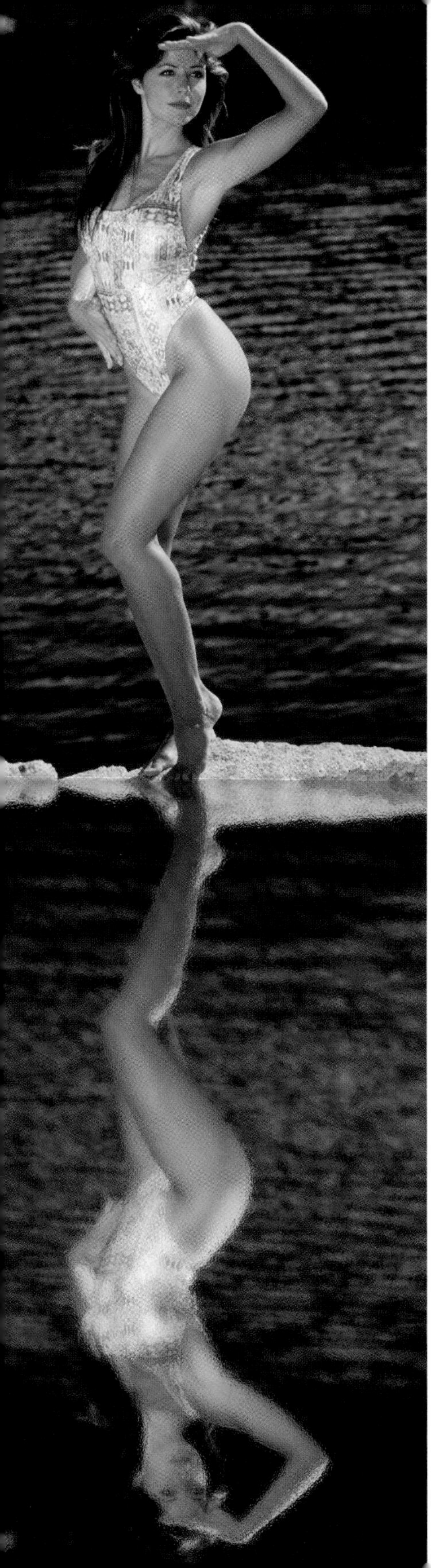

◀ FIGURE 3.112

Tech info: Canon EOS 1v, Canon 70-200mm zoom @ 200mm. Exposure: 1/250 sec. @ f/22. ISO 200.

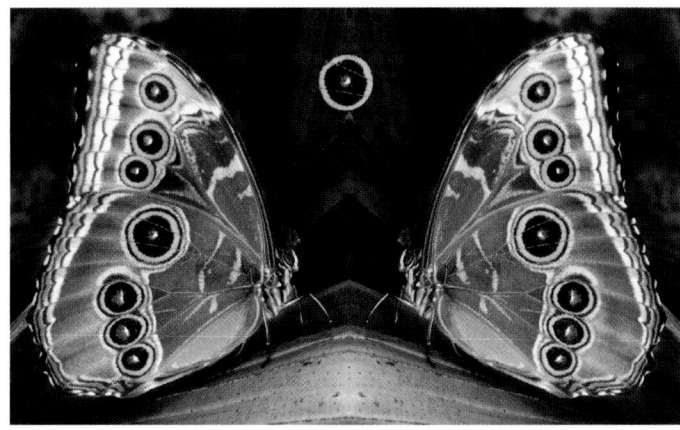

▲ FIGURE 3.113

Tech info: Canon EOS 1D, Canon 50mm Macro lens, Canon Macro Ring Lite MR-14EX. Exposure: 1/60 sec. @ f/22. ISO 100.

A Quick Pencil Sketch

This lesson is just for fun—like many of the others in the book. I like to have fun in Photoshop, as well as use its powerful imaging capabilities to enhance my professional photographs. I'll show you how I created an image that looks like I sketched it with a pencil on white paper.

I'll use a picture I took of a seagull in St. Augustine, Florida (Figure 3.114). Note that this effect, like many others you can create in Photoshop, works on some images better than others.

With the Layers dialog box open (Window > Layers), I created a duplicate layer (Figure 3.115). You can create a new layer using either of the following techniques: go to Layer > New Layer > Layer via Copy (press Command-J: Mac or Ctrl-J: Win), or drag the background layer down to the "Create a new layer" icon, which is what I did here.

▲ FIGURE 3.114

Tech info: Canon EOS 1D Mark II, Canon 100-400mm IS lens @ 4200mm. Exposure: 1/250 sec. @ f/8. ISO 200.

FIGURE 3.115

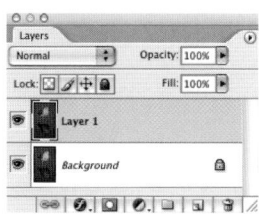

FIGURE 3.116

FIGURE 3.117

With the new (top) layer active (shaded in blue) (**Figure 3.116**), I went to Image > Adjustments > Desaturate. The image now appeared in black and white (**Figure 3.117**).

Next, I duplicated the top layer (you can use any of the afore-mentioned techniques). I now had a three-layer document (**Figure 3.118**).

Working on the top layer, I chose Image > Adjustments > Invert (press Command-I: Mac or Ctrl-I: Win). The file now looked like a negative (**Figure 3.119**).

While still working on the top layer, I selected Color Dodge mode from the pop-up menu at top left (**Figure 3.120**). The image almost totally disappeared, which is the normal result (**Figure 3.121**).

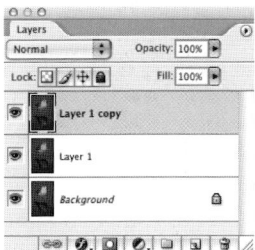

FIGURE 3.118

FIGURE 3.119

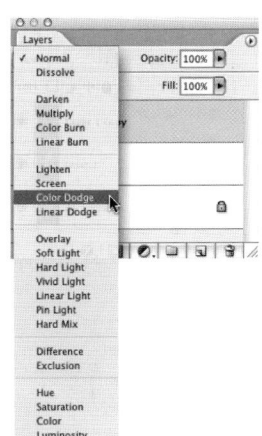

FIGURE 3.120

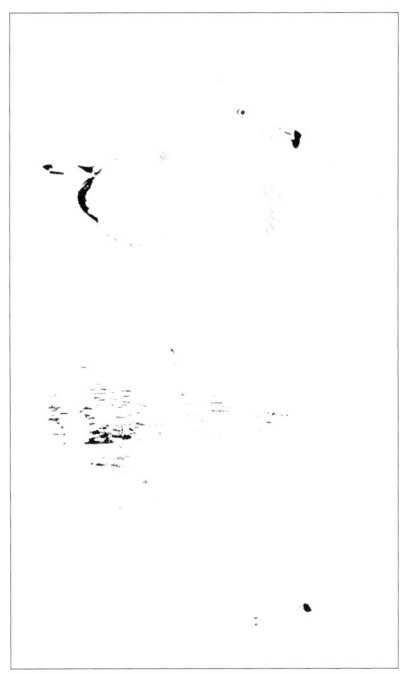

FIGURE 3.121

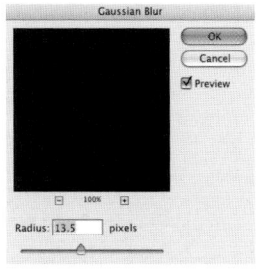

FIGURE 3.122

Still on the top layer, I went to Filter > Blur > Gaussian Blur and adjusted the Radius slider until I was pleased with how the pencil sketch image looked (**Figures 3.122** and **3.123**).

Just in case you thought this effect was only for the birds, here's how the same technique transformed another picture I took in St. Augustine into a pencil sketch (**Figures 3.124** and **3.125**).

Have fun, as always!

◀ FIGURE 3.123

▲ FIGURES 3.124 and 3.125 ▶

Tech info: Canon EOS 1Ds Mark II, Canon 17-40mm lens @ 17mm. Exposure: 1/125 sec. @ f/8. ISO 100.

Posterize an Image

Technically speaking, the Posterize adjustment in Photoshop is designed to analyze the pixel colors of a selected area of an image and reduce the number of colors, while maintaining the look of the original image. Visually, applying this adjustment makes photos look like wood block color artwork.

▼ FIGURE 3.126

Tech info: Canon EOS 1D Mark II, Canon 16-35mm lens @ 20mm. Exposure: 1/125 sec. @ f/11. ISO 100.

The Posterize adjustment is easy and fun to use. I'll show you how this adjustment affects one of my pictures of a model on South Beach, Miami (**Figure 3.126**).

First, I chose Image > Adjustments> Posterize to open this simple dialog box (**Figure 3.127**). You can change the effect by typing a different number in the Levels box; I selected 4. At first, you may be thrilled with the default setting, but I encourage you to play around with the different possibilities. You may be pleasantly surprised at what you'll come up with.

Here you see the effect of level 4 applied to my full-color image (**Figure 3.128**).

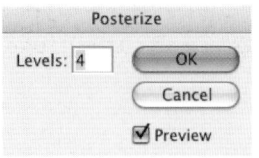

FIGURE 3.127

FIGURE 3.128

FIGURE 3.129

FIGURE 3.130

Next, I'll show you how the Posterize adjustment affected the sunset picture of a camel and rider that I worked with earlier in the chapter (**Figure 3.129**). I like the straight shot, but I thought you might like to see how the image looks when it's posterized. Here's the effect of level 4 on my color image (**Figure 3.130**). Cool! And here's the effect of level 4 on a black-and-white version of the same image (**Figure 3.131**).

Even after you've chosen a setting that you're pleased with, experiment with Curves, Levels, Filters, and so on to see how you can further enhance a picture. Remember: In Photoshop, a picture is never finished.

For example, here's a straight shot of a hotel in South Beach (**Figure 3.132**). I enhanced the image using Posterize, level 3 (**Figure 3.133**). After playing around with a few adjustments and filters, I decided to apply Warming Filter 85 (Image > Adjustments > Photo Filter > Warming Filter 85) with the Density setting at 100% (**Figure 3.134**). My image took on a totally new look (**Figure 3.135**).

FIGURE 3.131

▲ FIGURE 3.132

Tech info: Canon EOS 1D Mark II, Canon 16-35mm lens @ 24mm. Exposure: 1/60 sec. @ f/5.6.

◀ FIGURE 3.133

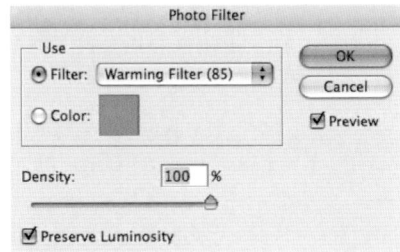

▲ FIGURE 3.134

▼ FIGURE 3.135

When you're applying the Posterize adjustment to an image, remember to keep it fun. In some cases, you (and your friends) may prefer the original color image. However, the Posterize adjustment can make a picture look more creative. Just ask Peter Max (www.petermax.com), the artist who gained fame in the 1960s with his colorful posterized pop art.

As long as I'm talking about posterizing an image, I'll mention *solarizing*. Here's how the Solarize filter (Filter > Stylize > Solarize) affected the previous image (**Figure 3.136**). My message, again, is that an image is never finished in Photoshop!

FIGURE 3.136

4 Advanced-Image Artistry

YOU'VE MADE IT to the most difficult and most complicated part of this book. Only kidding! The artistic techniques presented in this chapter are, indeed, more advanced than those on the previous pages; however, the lessons here have an underlying theme: fun! Keep the fun aspect of Photoshop in mind, and "working" on an image becomes "playing" with the image.

If you're new to Photoshop and feel overwhelmed by all the creative tools and options, here is a little story that may help you, as it did me. In Anne Lamont's wonderful book on writing, *Bird by Bird*, she recounts an anecdote from her childhood. Her brother is working on a school project about birds—the birds' markings, songs, habitats, and so on. The boy is overwhelmed and close to tears. He doesn't know where to begin! The project, which he had months to prepare, is due the next day. Their father looks at all the unopened books, papers, binders, and notes, and listens to his son explain his dilemma. "Son," he says, "bird by bird, buddy. Just take it bird by bird." My Photoshop friends, take each lesson bird by bird.

LET YOUR IMAGINATION SOAR.

Creative Explorations

Artistic Photoshop images can be created from mundane snapshots. However, starting with an artistic photograph gives you a creative edge, because the picture already looks imaginative as a straight shot.

▼ FIGURE 4.1

Tech info: Canon EOS 1D Mark II, 16-35mm lens @ 16mm. Exposure: 1/30 sec. @ f/4.5. ISO 1000.

We'll lead off this lesson with some creative enhancements I made to a photograph I took during an impromptu photo session in a small art-deco hotel in Miami's South Beach.

Here's a wide-angle look at the setting (**Figure 4.1**). The light level was extremely low. I could have used a flash, but the harsh light from the flash would have destroyed the mood of the setting. So, I used a high ISO (1000) and took an available-light, handheld picture.

Figure 4.2 is my favorite image from the photo session. It's a much tighter shot. Let me show you just a few of the creative enhancements I explored.

Looking for interesting adjustments, I came upon Threshold (Image > Adjustments > Threshold). After I selected Threshold, I adjusted the effect with the Threshold slider (**Figure 4.3**). Here's the effect of applying Threshold to my image (**Figure 4.4**). The picture looks like a lithograph, but it's not exactly what I had in mind. As usual, I wanted to see the effect of fading the filter. So, after applying Threshold, I chose Edit > Fade Threshold. To soften the Threshold effect, I reduced the layer's Opacity to 40% (**Figure 4.5**). (It's an Adjustment Layer, remember?) Reducing the Opacity gave me a custom Threshold effect (**Figure 4.6**). You can play around with fading any effect or filter to create your own custom effects; there are endless possibilities.

▲ FIGURE 4.2

Tech info: Canon EOS 1D Mark II, 28-105mm lens
@ 105mm. Exposure: 1/30 sec. @ f/4.5. ISO 1000.

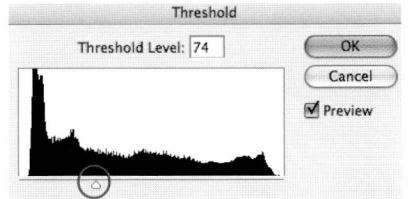

FIGURE 4.3

FIGURE 4.4

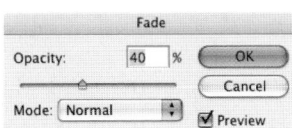

FIGURE 4.5

FIGURE 4.6

In Photoshop, one of the many filters that add a creative touch to a picture is the Diffuse Glow filter (Filter > Distort > Diffuse Glow) (**Figure 4.7**). As with all of the program's filters, I recommend playing with the sliders to produce your own custom creations.

For my final image, I applied the Diffuse Glow filter to my original image. Then, I added the Emulsion Frame found in PhotoFrame Pro 3.0, a collection of Photoshop-compatible plug-ins from onOne Software (www.ononesoftware.com) (**Figure 4.8**).

It's your turn to experiment with your own creative Photoshop explorations.

FIGURE 4.7

FIGURE 4.8

Art History Brush 101

The Art History Brush gives you the creativity to "hand paint" an image in a unique and original way, because you can choose from dozens of brushes, brush styles, and brush sizes. What's more, the speed at which you paint, fast or slow, affects the painterly result.

So, unlike a Photoshop filter, which applies an effect to the entire image, the Art History Brush lets you apply an effect to select areas of a picture.

Let's begin with a picture I took of a bleeding heart blossom—one of Mother Nature's artistic creations (**Figure 4.9**). The Art History Brush is nested in the Tool Bar with the History Brush (**Figure 4.10**). After I selected the Art History Brush, it was time to select a brush. The style you select is very important: You want to select a brush that simulates a brush an artist would use. To begin, I clicked the blue pop-down menu next to the Brush window on the Menu Bar at the top of the monitor (**Figure 4.11**). Doing so opened the Brushes palette. Then, I used the scroll bar to scroll down until I found a brush

▲ FIGURE 4.9

Tech info: Canon EOS 1Ds Mark II, 50mm Macro lens. Exposure: 1/30 sec. @ f/8. ISO 200.

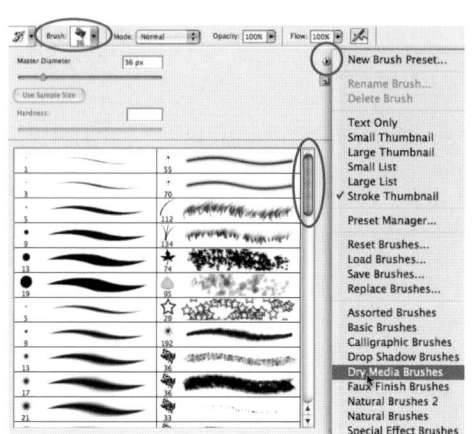

FIGURE 4.11

FIGURE 4.10

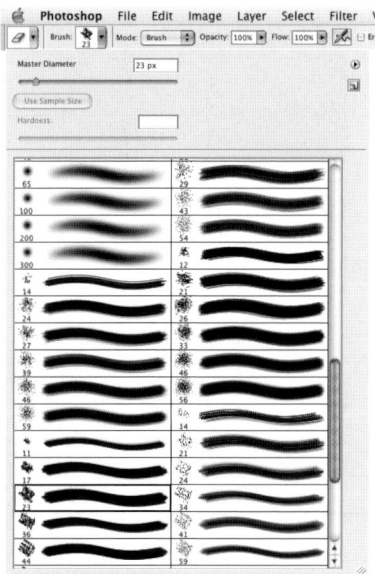

FIGURE 4.12

I liked. For a choice of truly artistic brushes, click the little fly-out arrow in the Brushes palette; doing so reveals a long menu of creative brushes. In this case, I clicked Dry Media Brushes.

NOTE: *Before I could use the new brushes, I had to load them. When I clicked the new brushes, a window opened, asking whether I wanted to Append (add to) the existing brushes, Replace the current brushes, or Cancel. I recommend clicking Append; that way, your existing brushes (default or other loaded brushes) remain untouched, and the new brushes are added below the existing brushes for easy access.*

Here's a partial view of my Brushes window, showing the newly added brushes (**Figure 4.12**). What a choice! Again, you can use the scroll bar to see other brushes.

More creative options await you. On the Menu Bar, you can choose a style. Play around with the different styles to see which ones fit your artistic needs.

Here you see my choices for using the Art History Brush on my bleeding heart blossom image: Dry Media Brush 63 and Tight Short (**Figure 4.13**).

After I spent about five minutes painting my picture with the Art History Brush, my image was transformed into a more artistic picture (**Figure 4.14**).

FIGURE 4.14

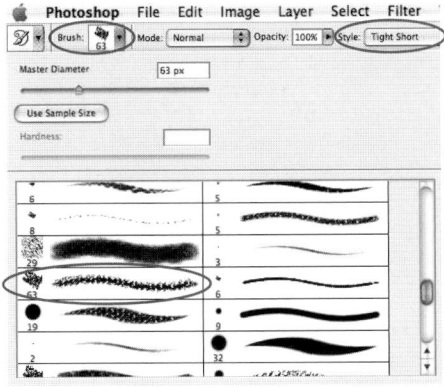

FIGURE 4.13

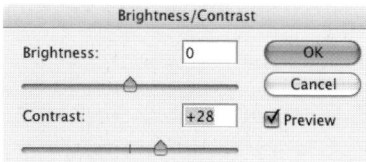

FIGURE 4.15

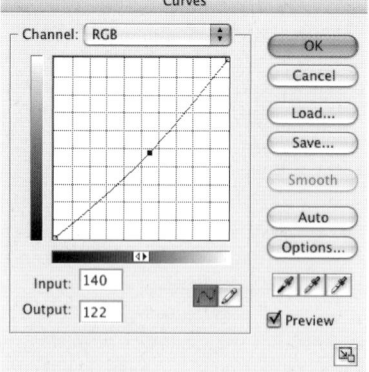

FIGURE 4.16

But wait! The picture looked a little flat. So, I boosted the contrast just a bit by going to Image > Adjustments > Brightness/Contrast (**Figure 4.15**). Then, I darkened the picture by going to Image > Adjustments > Curves and pulling down the curve line (**Figure 4.16**).

After making the additional Contrast and Curves adjustments, I was pleased with my image (**Figure 4.17**).

As I mentioned, it helps to start your Art History Brush creation with an artistic image (**Figure 4.18**). Here's one more example of how you can transform a photograph using this creative tool (**Figure 4.19**).

I hate to leave you with a poor example of using the Art History Brush, but I want to make an important point. When you're applying a brush, select one that's very small. If you select a large brush, your image will be blurred, and it will be difficult to recognize the original subject (**Figure 4.20**). However, all art is subjective, and there may be someone out there who likes this result. (By the way, if you turn this page upside down and look at the image in a dark room illuminated only by a candle, you'll find the answer to why Paul McCartney isn't wearing shoes on the cover of The Beatles' *Abbey Road* album.)

◀ FIGURE 4.17

▲ FIGURE 4.18

Tech info: Canon EOS 1Ds Mark II, 50mm Macro lens. Exposure: 1/125 sec. @ f/8. ISO 100.

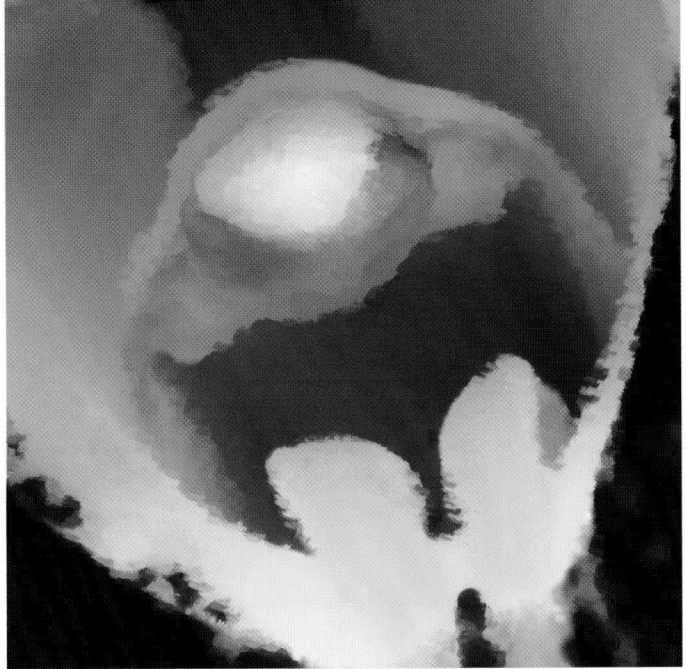

FIGURE 4.19

FIGURE 4.20

◀ FIGURES 4.21 and 4.22

Tech info: Canon EOS 1D Mark II, Canon 50mm Macro lens. Exposure: 1/60 sec. @ f/16. ISO 100.

I changed my mind about using a poor illustration for the last image in this lesson. Here's a nice set of images that illustrates the creative power of the Art History Brush (**Figures 4.21** and **4.22**).

Put on your painter's cap—and your thinking cap—and start painting with the Art History Brush.

An Illuminating Lighting Effect

In this lesson, we'll look at an effect that is amazing, creative, and fun. In Adobe Photoshop CS2, you can change the direction and type of the lighting in a photograph with the Lighting Effects filter (Filter > Render > Lighting Effects). You can transform a picture with flat lighting into a picture in which the subject looks as though he (or she, or it) was photographed in a spotlight or another type of light with a narrow beam. How cool is that! This effect works well for portraits and still-life photographs. Let's turn on the lights.

▼ FIGURE 4.23

Tech info: Canon EOS 1D Mark II, Canon 28-105mm lens @ 105mm. Exposure 1/125 sec. @ f/5.6. ISO 400.

I took this photograph of my friend Chandler deep within the Amazon rain forest (**Figure 4.23**). Only kidding! I snapped this picture at Jungle World, an exhibit at New York's Bronx Zoo that recreates a jungle. I like the picture, but I knew more dramatic lighting possibilities awaited me in Photoshop. Basically, I wanted to create the effect that Chandler was in the rain forest and illuminated by light streaming through an opening in the forest's thick canopy.

The first step was to go to Filter > Render > Lighting Effects. When you open the Lighting Effects dialog box, you'll see all the available creative choices, giving you limitless creative control over the effects. (Don't panic!) To make things simple for first-time visitors to Lighting Effects, I've put a few indicators on my screenshot of the dialog box (**Figure 4.24**). The red arrow indicates that I selected Omni as my Light Type. The larger ovals show where you control the Intensity and Exposure—two of the most important controls in Lighting Effects. On the left side of the dialog box, the Preview window shows how the Lighting Effects will be applied to your picture. The red circles show anchor points that let you change the size of the circle in Omni light. As the size of the circle changes, so does the intensity of the Lighting Effects.

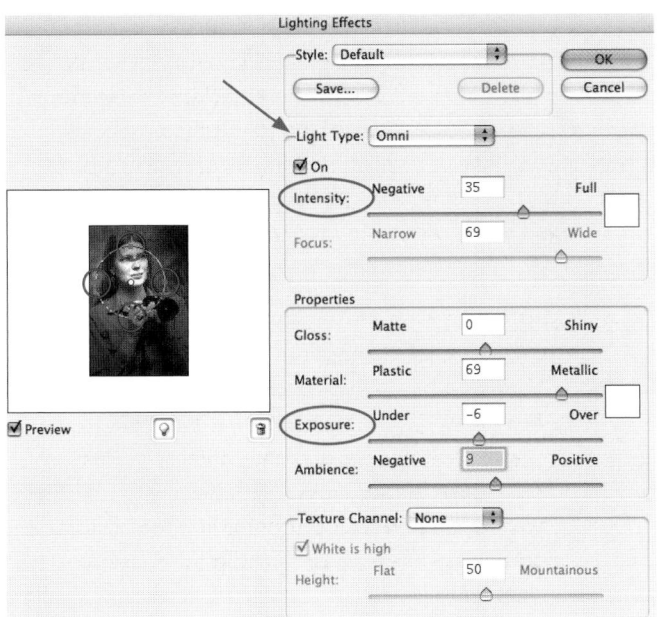

FIGURE 4.24

FIGURE 4.25

Here you see the result of the Lighting Effects filter being applied with my personal settings (**Figure 4.25**). The area surrounding Chandler is darker; that's the effect I wanted. However, the area around Chandler's mouth is now washed out and overexposed. It looks like Chandler has a bad sunburn—but I cured it in a flash.

To darken that area, I chose Edit > Fade Lighting Effects. The default Fade mode is Normal. Had I selected the Normal mode and reduced the filter's effect using the Opacity slider, I would have faded the effect for the entire image—something I didn't want to do. To darken only the overexposed area of Chandler's face, I chose the Darken mode, which darkened only the washed-out area of the photograph (**Figure 4.26**).

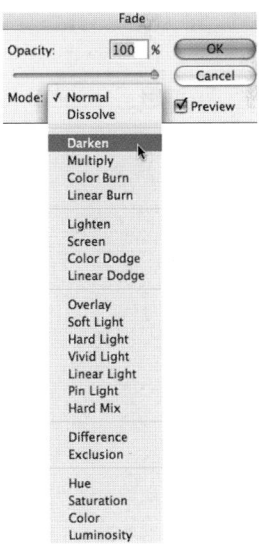

FIGURE 4.26

FIGURE 4.27

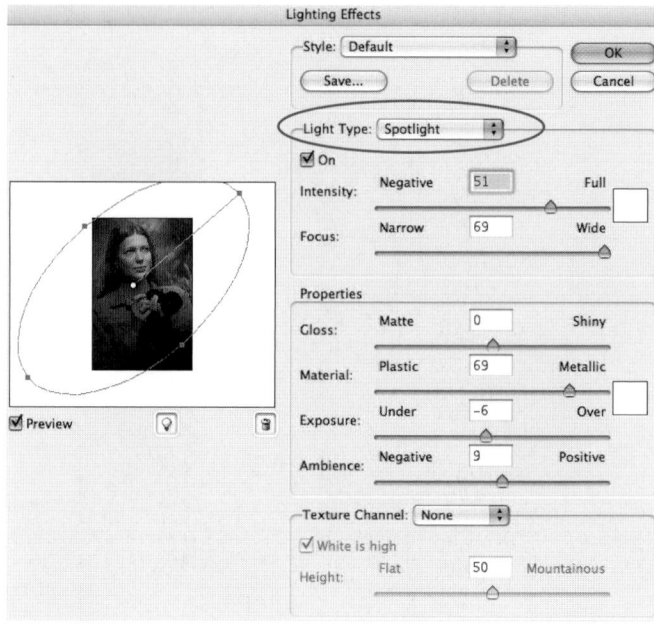

FIGURE 4.28

When you're fading a filter, play with the different modes, along with the Opacity slider, to see their effects on your picture.

That's it! Chandler's "sunburn" has been eliminated, and the flat lighting has been replaced with lighting that's a bit more artistic (**Figure 4.27**).

Spotlight is another of my favorite Lighting Effects. As you can see in this screenshot, an oval appears around Chandler in the Preview window, rather than the circle in the Omni effect (**Figure 4.28**). As before, you can use the anchor points to change the quality and intensity of the light, but here you can also change the direction of the light by swiveling the oval in any direction.

After some experimentation with Lighting Effects, I found just the effect I wanted (**Figure 4.29**).

Again, don't panic when you open the Lighting Effects dialog box. Take your time, put on some music, and play with this cool and creative effect. I'm sure you'll find it very illuminating.

▶ FIGURE 4.29

▼ FIGURES 4.30 and 4.31

Tech info: Canon EOS 1Ds
Mark II, 17-40mm lens @
17mm. Exposure: 1/125 sec.
@ f/16. ISO 100.

Black-and-White and Beyond

First-time Photoshop CS2 users often create black-and-white images from their color files by converting them to grayscale images (Image > Mode > Grayscale). That technique is quick and easy, and it can produce OK images, especially when Levels, Curves, and/or Contrast adjustments are applied to the converted file. The accompanying color and grayscale images illustrate that technique (**Figures 4.30** and **4.31**).

Photoshop CS2 offers several other methods for creating a range of black-and-white image conversions—more dramatic images with a greater tonal range. Let's look at a few of these options and then explore how to go beyond producing simple grayscale images.

Another easy (but more creative) way to create a black-and-white image is to use Camera Raw (**Figures 4.32**, **4.33**, and **4.34**). In the Adjust tab, remove all the color using the Saturation slider. Then play around with the other controls, beginning with Contrast in this tab (uncheck the Auto box first). For more creative control, go to the Curve tab and fine-tune the picture to your liking.

▼ FIGURE 4.32

Tech info: Canon EOS 1Ds Mark II,
17-40mm lens @ 17mm. Exposure: 1/125
sec. @ f/16. ISO 100.

Canon EOS–1D Mark II: HW5U1613.CR2 (ISO 100, 1/100, f/18, 17–40@25 mm)

☑ Preview ☑ Shadows ☑ Highlights   R: --- G: --- B: ---

Settings: Custom

Adjust Detail Lens Curve Calibrate

White Balance: As Shot

Temperature   4800
Tint   +8

Exposure   ☐ Auto   +0.70
Shadows   ☐ Auto   0
Brightness   ☐ Auto   50
Contrast   ☐ Auto   +25
Saturation   -100

19.3%

☑ Show Workflow Options

Space: ProPhoto RGB   Size: 3504 by 2336 (8.2 MP)
Depth: 8 Bits/Channel   Resolution: 240   pixels/inch

Save...   Cancel
Open   Done

▲ FIGURES 4.33 and 4.34 ▼

▲ FIGURE 4.35

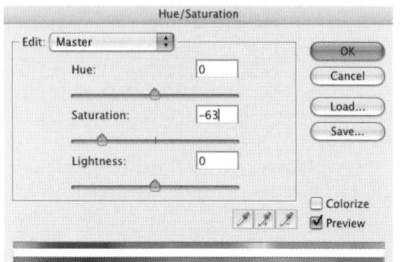

◄ FIGURE 4.36

Before I started this lesson, I promised myself I'd stick to the straight enhancements. Well, I didn't get far. My cowboy picture begged for a tried-and-proven enhancement (useful for either a black-and-white or a color image): darkening the grass with the Burn tool to draw more attention to the main subjects (**Figure 4.35**). I'll stick to my guns from here on in, partner, even though I'd normally make additional enhancements (burning, dodging, selectively applying Levels, Curves, and so on) to the following images.

Getting back to desaturating an image, you can remove all of the color, or just some of it, by using the Saturation slider in Hue/Saturation (Image > Adjustments > Hue/Saturation) (**Figure 4.36**).

Note how this less-saturated version of my cowboy picture has a softer feel than the full-color image (**Figure 4.37**).

▼ FIGURE 4.37

I photographed this woman in Old Havana, Cuba, in 2000 with my Canon D30 and Canon 16-35mm lens (Figure 4.38). I love the way the color of the blue Chevy and the woman's clothes complement each other.

Compare these two photographs (Figures 4.39 and 4.40). One is a grayscale image (Image > Mode > Grayscale). I created the other using Channel Mixer (Image > Adjustments > Channel Mixer). Which do you feel looks more dramatic? That's right—*not* the grayscale image.

When you select Channel Mixer (as an Adjustment Layer, Layer > New Adjustment Layer > Channel Mixer) and check the Monochrome box, you can control the Red, Green, and Blue Source Channels to fine-tune the image to your creative vision.

▲ FIGURE 4.38

Tech info: Canon EOS D30, 16-35mm lens @ 35mm. Exposure: 1/125 sec. @ f/8. ISO 400.

FIGURE 4.39

FIGURE 4.40

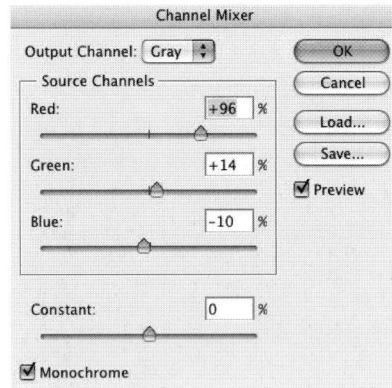

FIGURE 4.41

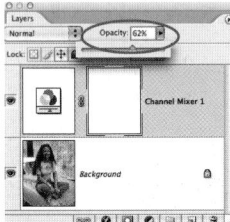

FIGURE 4.42

Here are the Channel Mixer settings I used on my color picture (**Figure 4.41**):

- Red: +96%
- Green: +14%
- Blue: −10%

Combine my settings, and you get 100%. That's no accident. All three channels together shouldn't exceed 100%—if you go over 100%, you overexpose the image; and if you go under 100%, you underexpose the image. That said, who's to say you can't tweak an image for a desired effect?

I don't use the Constant control in the Channel Mixer dialog box because it can make the image look flat. But if you want, you can move the Constant slider to the left to darken the image or to the right to lighten the image. Negative values add more black, and positive values add more white.

Play around with Channel Mixer once, and you'll never make a grayscale conversion again. For additional creativity after using Channel Mixer, try the Curves or Levels commands.

If you use the Channel Mixer Adjustment Layer, try fading the layer's Opacity. Here, I reduced the Opacity to 62% (**Figure 4.42**).

This is the result (**Figure 4.43**). The once-vibrant colors are now more subdued, and the picture looks more creative.

At first, this may look like a black-and-white picture (**Figure 4.44**). Actually, it's a duotone (I chose Image > Mode > Grayscale and then Image > Mode > Duotone).

A true duotone is a black-and-white image to which another color is added. Duotone images are often used in magazines and books when a four-color page isn't available, as well as for creating pictures with a different look. Duotones

◀ FIGURE 4.43

are also used for posters and in fine-art exhibits. Several of Ansel Adams' posters are duotones.

For the duotone image of my Cuban friend, I clicked the Load button and selected Pantone 478 CVC from the Duotones folder. You can find this folder and lots more like it in the Presets folder inside the Photoshop folder.

After applying that color, I clicked the small Curve window to the left of the Ink color window. Doing so brought up the Duotone Curve window, where I made my adjustments (**Figure 4.45**).

Photoshop groups Duotones along with Tritones (three ink colors) and Quadtones (that's right, four ink colors) in the Duotone Options dialog box. The color of the ink is displayed, so it's relatively easy to visualize how the color will affect the image (**Figure 4.46**).

TIP: To see all the Duotone options, you need to load the other inks. To do so, click the Load button in the Duotone Options dialog box. In the resulting Load dialog box, you can load additional colors.

FIGURE 4.44

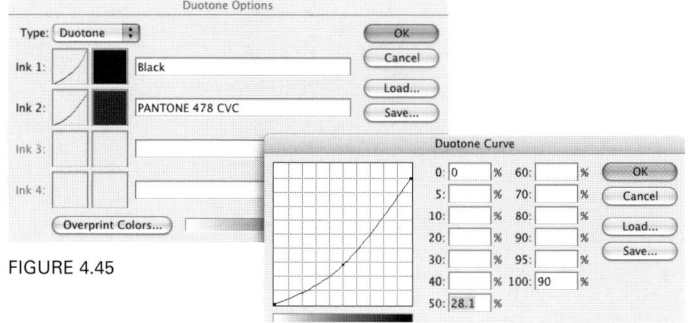

FIGURE 4.45

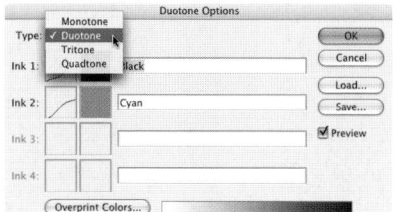

FIGURE 4.46

Another Black-and-White Approach

You can also create a customized black-and-white image in Photoshop with the B/W Conversion filter found in Nik's Color Efex Pro (www.niksoftware.com). When you select this Photoshop-compatible plug-in, you can quickly see the effect of different color filters on your picture (**Figure 4.47**). It's like putting a different color filter over a lens when shooting black-and-white film, but here you use a slider to simulate the filter's effect.

You can also adjust the image's brightness and contrast. Of course, you can make additional adjustments in Photoshop CS2 using Curves and Levels, and by using Fade (Edit > Fade B/W Filter).

Here's the effect of the Nik B/W filter applied to the picture of the deserted homestead that led off this lesson (**Figure 4.48**).

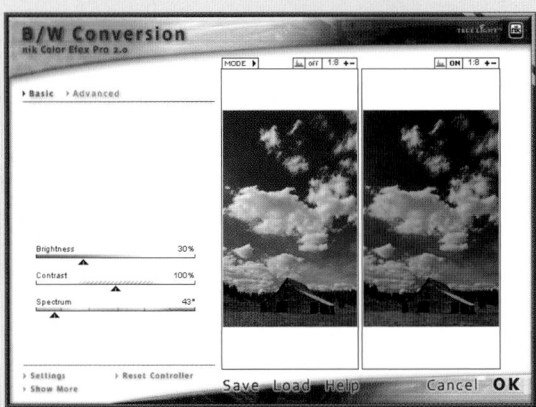

FIGURE 4.47

FIGURE 4.48

Go Beyond the Visible Light Spectrum

Compare the color image in this series to the other two (**Figures 4.49**, **4.50**, and **4.51**). One is a grayscale image. The much more dramatic picture is an infrared (IR) image.

Some digital cameras offer IR capabilities when a Hoya R72 filter is placed over the lens, and several Photoshop plug-ins offer an IR filter, including Nik's Color Efex Pro. Personally, the most realistic IR images I've seen have been produced by cameras that have been converted to shoot only infrared (see www.irdigital.net).

I took my converted D60 on a trip out West (this picture was taken in Bryce Canyon, Utah) and after viewing the pictures on my laptop each night, I started to "see" the landscapes in infrared.

▲ FIGURE 4.49

Tech info: Canon EOS 1Ds Mark II, 17-40mm lens @ 20mm. Exposure: 1/125 sec. @ f/16. ISO 100.

FIGURE 4.50

▲ FIGURE 4.51

Tech info: Canon EOS D60 converted to IR-only camera, 17-40mm lens @ 17mm. Exposure: 1/30 sec. @ f/22. ISO 50.

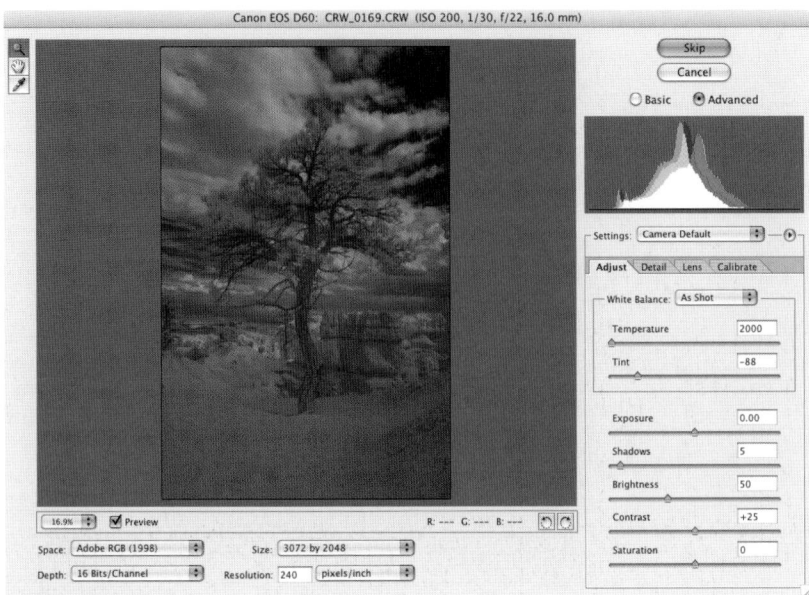

Canon EOS D60: CRW_0169.CRW (ISO 200, 1/30, f/22, 16.0 mm)

FIGURE 4.52

Straight out of an IR-converted camera, the pictures have a purple tint (**Figure 4.52**). To get the IR effect, you need to desaturate the image and adjust Levels to your liking. To maximize image quality, you must shoot in raw and use 16-bit depth.

Another technique for going beyond black-and-white is to simulate a black-and-white infrared picture. To do so in this case, I converted a color file to a grayscale image (Image > Mode > Grayscale) and then applied the Diffuse Glow filter (Filter > Distort > Diffuse Glow) to the image (**Figures 4.53** and **4.54**). If the effect is too intense, you can fade the effect, as you can fade any filter, by choosing Edit > Fade Diffuse Glow (**Figure 4.55**).

Enough tech talk. Let's chat for a moment about why we like black-and-white photography. Perhaps a black-and-white picture, such as this street scene from Trinidad, Cuba, on the next page, looks more creative than a color picture (**Figure 4.56**). By removing the color from the scene and therefore removing some of the scene's reality, perhaps you're able to use your imagination more. Because the picture can't use color to draw you into the scene, perhaps the subject must be more interesting. Perhaps it just looks cool. Whatever the reason, I think you'll have fun exploring the creative options of black-and-white photography.

▼ FIGURE 4.53

Tech info: Canon EOS 1Ds Mark II, 50mm Macro lens. Exposure: 1/15 sec. @ f/22. ISO 100.

Diffuse Glow (33.3%)

FIGURE 4.54

FIGURE 4.55

▶ FIGURE 4.56

Tech info: Canon EOS D30,
16-35mm lens @ 20mm. Exposure:
1/125 sec. @ f/5.6. ISO 400.

▲ FIGURE 4.57

Tech info: Canon EOS
1Ds Mark II, 15mm lens.
Exposure: 1/60 sec. @ f/8.
ISO 100.

Color and Black-and-White Together

In Photoshop CS2, it's easy to create a black-and-white and color image—that is, an image in which some of the elements are in black-and-white and some are in color. It's all done with layers; here's how.

I'll show you how I worked (played) with a picture I took on the Ponderosa Ranch in Seneca, Oregon. It's a full-color image, as you can see (**Figure 4.57**).

My first step was to create a duplicate layer in the Layers palette. Next, I turned off the top layer (the Background copy) by clicking the eye icon next to it (**Figure 4.58**). I clicked the bottom layer to activate it. Then, I chose Image > Adjustments > Hue/Saturation and moved the Saturation slider all the way to the left to totally desaturate the bottom layer (**Figure 4.59**).

I clicked the top layer to activate it (**Figure 4.60**). Keep in mind that the top layer is a color layer and the bottom layer is basically a black-and-white layer now, even though it's still RGB. Next, I chose the Eraser tool on the Tool Bar, adjusted my brush size with the bracket keys on my keyboard (the left bracket makes the brush smaller, the right bracket makes the brush larger), and erased the picture's background. To show the white background color, turn off the bottom layer

FIGURE 4.58

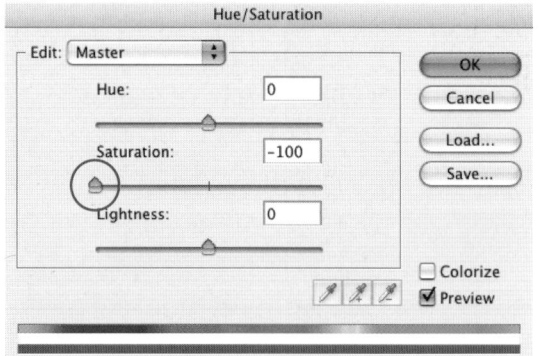

FIGURE 4.59

FIGURE 4.60

by clicking the eye icon. I like to do that so I have a good idea of what I've erased, what still needs to be erased, and what I may have erased in error (**Figure 4.61**). To see the black-and-white and color versions merged, turn the bottom layer back on.

Here's the result (**Figure 4.62**). The main subject is in color, and the background is in black-and-white.

FIGURE 4.61

FIGURE 4.62

Hand-Color a Black-and-White Image

When I was kid, my mother hand-colored my dad's black-and-white photographs using a fine brush and small tubes of oil paint. Before my eyes, grayscale images that had been developed in our basement darkroom were turned into colorful, artistic, one-of-a-kind creations.

In Photoshop CS2, you can simulate the popular and satisfying hand-coloring technique of the 1950s—but more quickly, and with endless colors from which to choose. Plus, if you make a mistake, you can fix it immediately by using the History palette to go back in time. What's more, even after you finish your masterpiece, you can repair a mistake or change your mind about a color by deleting a color layer and adding a new one.

Before you begin exploring these techniques, a word of advice: Try them when you have plenty of time. Put on some music. Relax. Enjoy the process. Let your creative juices flow.

For this lesson, I'll use a picture I took of my son, Marco, playing a guitar in a local music store (**Figure 4.63**). Although it looks like a grayscale file, it's actually an RGB file taken with my digital SLR set to the black-and-white mode. Note that you must work with an RBG or CMYK file when

▶ FIGURE 4.63

Tech info: Canon EOS 1Ds Mark II, 16-35mm lens. Exposure: 1/30 sec. @ f/5.6. ISO 800.

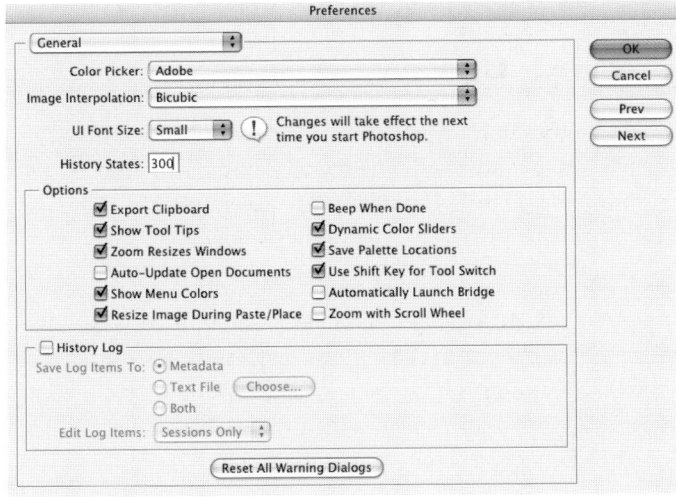

FIGURE 4.64

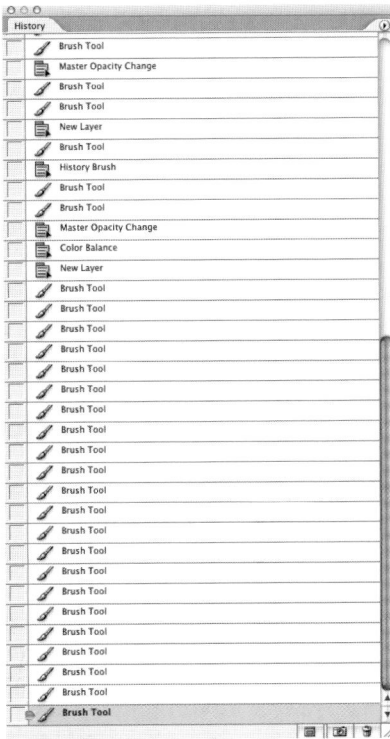

FIGURE 4.65

you're hand-coloring; adding a color layer isn't an option when you work on a true grayscale file.

My first step in this process, as it is in any process that involves many steps, was to increase the number of History States in Photoshop's Preferences (Photoshop > Preferences > General). I entered 300 in the History States field (**Figure 4.64**). I went a little nuts here, because I knew I was going to spend a lot of time on the image.

Once my History States were set, I opened the History palette (Window > History) so I could keep track of each step and go back if necessary. My History palette looked like this after I worked on the image for just a few minutes (**Figure 4.65**).

Here's the key to hand-coloring a picture: I added a color layer by choosing Layer > New > Layer, and, in the New Layer dialog box that appears, selecting Color from the Mode pop-up menu and leaving the Opacity at 100% (**Figure 4.66**). If you try to paint on a standard layer, you'll cover all the detail in the area you paint over. Now the color layer was on top of the Background layer in the Layers palette. It looks blank at first; it only has color in it when you paint in the color.

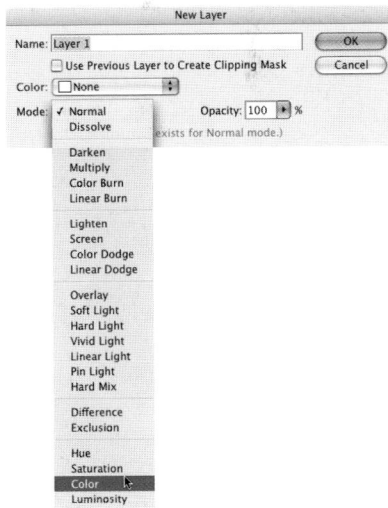

FIGURE 4.66

Next I selected a brush from the Tool Bar (**Figure 4.67**). I used the bracket keys on my keyboard to make the brush smaller (left bracket key) or larger (right bracket key).

It was almost time to start hand-coloring my picture. I knew that getting the color for the face would be a challenge. Here's how I did it. I opened another picture of Marco and used the Eyedropper tool in the Tool Bar to pick up the color from his face in that picture (**Figure 4.68**). The foreground color was now set to the color of my son's face.

The color wasn't exactly right, just as a skin tone from one of your pictures may not be perfect for use in another one (**Figure 4.69**). Applied to this image, the color of the skin was too saturated and too dark, and it needed a touch of yellow.

I fine-tuned the chosen color by reducing the Opacity of the color layer and by adjusting the colors in the Color Balance window (Image > Adjustments > Color Balance) (**Figures 4.70** and **4.71**). After I played around with these adjustments, the skin color was more natural, as you'll see in a bit.

With the skin tone dialed in, I began to hand-color the picture. After I finished hand-coloring my son's face and arms, I clicked the Foreground Color at the bottom of the Tool Bar to open the Color Picker, from which I chose my color (**Figure 4.72**). Then, I colored the guitar he was holding, his beret and shirt, and some of the guitars on the wall.

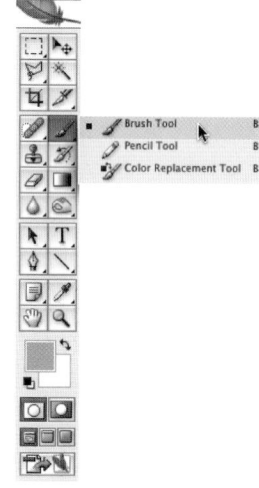

FIGURE 4.67

FIGURE 4.68

FIGURE 4.69

TIP: You can also choose a color from the Swatches palette (Window > Swatches).

You should keep the Layers palette open as you work. As you can see—and this is important—each color is on a different layer (**Figure 4.73**). If you change your mind about a color or make a mistake, you can trash that layer and create a new color layer without affecting the other colors and layers of your picture.

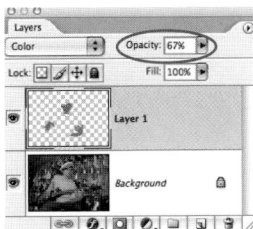

FIGURE 4.70

In the previous screenshot, you may have noticed that the eye icon on the Background layer (bottom layer) was turned off. Turning off that layer from time to time is a good idea because you can see whether you're doing a good job of hand-coloring your picture—or whether, as in this case, more work needs to be done (**Figure 4.74**).

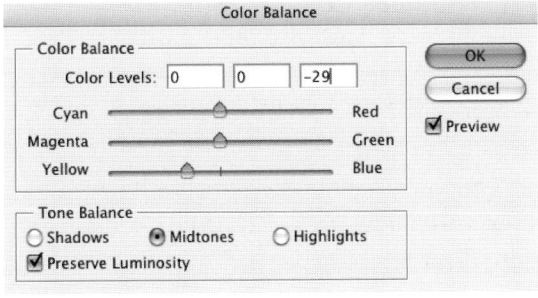

FIGURE 4.71

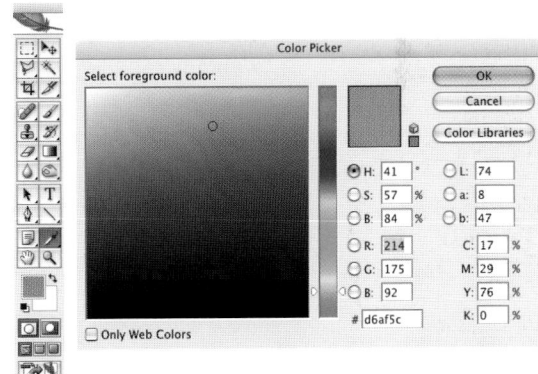

FIGURE 4.72

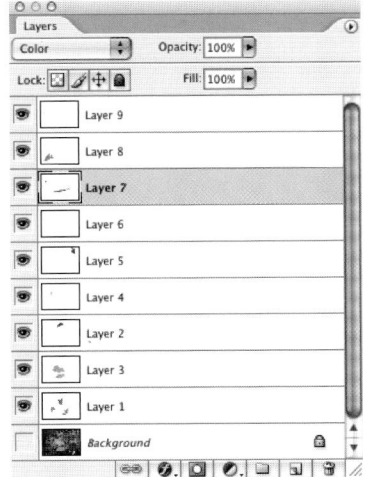

FIGURE 4.73

FIGURE 4.74

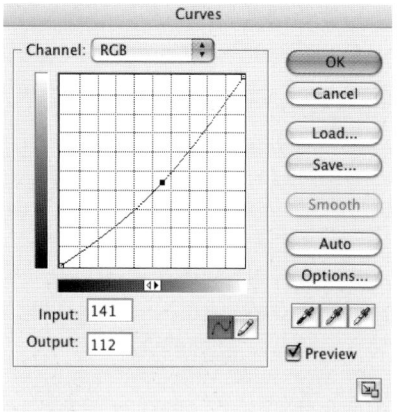

FIGURE 4.75

After completing my hand-painting process, I thought the picture looked too bright. So, I used Curves (Image > Adjustments > Curves) to darken the image by pulling down the Curve from the midpoint (**Figure 4.75**).

Here's my almost-finished image (**Figure 4.76**). I share this with you for the reason I stress repeatedly to my workshop students (and in this book): A picture is never finished in Photoshop, because there are endless creative possibilities.

My next step was to use Lens Flare (Filter > Render > Lens Flare) to simulate a bright light on the boring ceiling (**Figure 4.77**). Then, to reduce the brightness of the annoying white tag on the neck of the guitar, I selected that area with the Magic Wand tool on the Tool Bar and filled it with gray.

On the next page is my final hand-colored image (**Figure 4.78**). I wonder what my mother would think?

I've also included another version that I ran through the Midnight filter found in Nik Software's Color Efex Pro 2.0 (**Figure 4.79**). This picture is probably more to my son's liking—it looks as though he's playing in a way-cool guitar store with the lights turned down low.

FIGURE 4.76

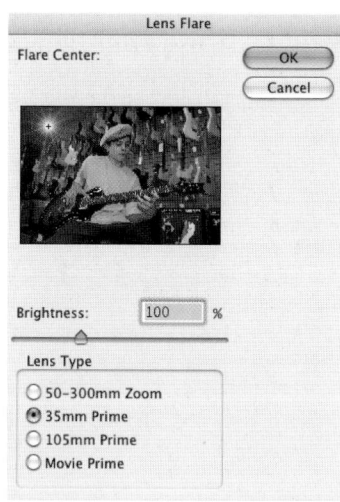

FIGURE 4.77

▲ FIGURES 4.78 and 4.79

Intensify Action

Getting a good sports action shot of a subject moving at relatively high speed requires choosing the correct shutter speed, selecting the correct aperture, carefully focusing and composing the picture, and then releasing the shutter at precisely the correct moment (or selecting rapid frame advance for a series of shots with the hope of getting a few keepers).

Having followed the correct techniques, I captured the opening picture for this lesson. (Hey, I know it needs some work! That's why I'm using it!)

▼ FIGURE 4.80

Tech info: Canon EOS 1D Mark II, 100-400mm IS lens @ 320mm. Exposure: 1/500 sec. @ f/8. ISO 400.

I'll begin by presenting some conventional digital enhancements of the picture, because that's part of the creative process (usually the first part). Then, you'll learn how you can intensify the action in a picture.

Sounds like fun. Let's go!

Here's a straight out-of-the-camera shot of Marco wake boarding (**Figure 4.80**).

To independently darken the shadow areas of the picture and lighten the subject, I used the Shadow/Highlight control (Image > Adjustments > Shadow/Highlight) (**Figure 4.81**).

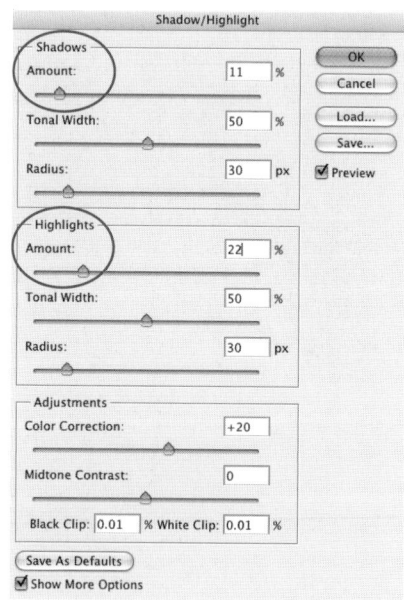

FIGURE 4.81

Now Marco's face is brighter (**Figure 4.82**). You'll also notice that the picture is cropped. After opening a picture, saving it, and working only on a copy of the picture (you should never work on an original), it's a good idea to crop it. That way, when you're experimenting with adjustments, areas of the picture that you'll eventually crop out won't influence those adjustments. So, I cropped the picture as my first step.

Marco has a nice tan on his lower arms and legs, but not where his t-shirt and shorts covered his body while he was in the sun. I thought it was time to give him an even tan. To do that, I first selected the Eyedropper tool and clicked the tanned part of his leg. Doing so set the Foreground Color to the tanned skin tone (**Figure 4.83**).

FIGURE 4.82

FIGURE 4.83

FIGURE 4.84

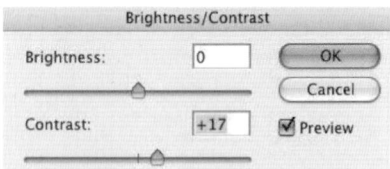

FIGURE 4.85

FIGURE 4.86

The next step was to add a color layer, just as I did in the previous lesson. (I needed to add a color layer because I couldn't color (paint) directly on a layer without blocking out details.) Next, I selected a brush from the Tool Bar and painted in the tan color on the lighter part of the boy's arms and legs. After giving the boy a tan, I flattened the layers (Layer > Flatten Image).

The picture was a bit flat (Figure 4.84). So, I boosted the Contrast (Image > Adjustments > Brightness/Contrast) to liven up the image (Figure 4.85).

Check out how the image looks after the boost in contrast (Figure 4.86). This is an improvement over simply using the Shadow/Highlight command.

FIGURE 4.87

I wasn't done with my basic enhancements. Next, I used the Burn tool to darken parts of the background and the Dodge tool to lighten Marco's face (even zooming in to lighten the white area of his eyes and his teeth). I also used the Clone Stamp tool to remove some of the distracting background objects (**Figure 4.87**).

To intensify the action of the picture, I first made a duplicate layer. Then, I applied the Radial Blur filter (Filter > Blur > Radial Blur), with the Zoom Blur Method selected, to the duplicate layer (**Figure 4.88**). I moved the center point of the blur directly over the point in the image area where Marco was positioned.

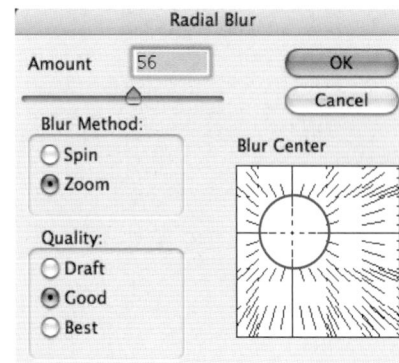

FIGURE 4.88

Next, I selected the Eraser tool and erased the blur over his body on the top layer (**Figure 4.89**). To see if I was doing a good (or bad) job with my erasing, I turned off the bottom layer by clicking the eye icon on that layer (**Figure 4.90**). As you can see, I needed to do more work!

The key to getting a smooth transition between the clear area and the blur area is to reduce the opacity of the Eraser tool on the Menu Bar as you move outward from the center of the subject (**Figure 4.91**). That reduction makes the transition between the blurred and sharp areas less noticeable.

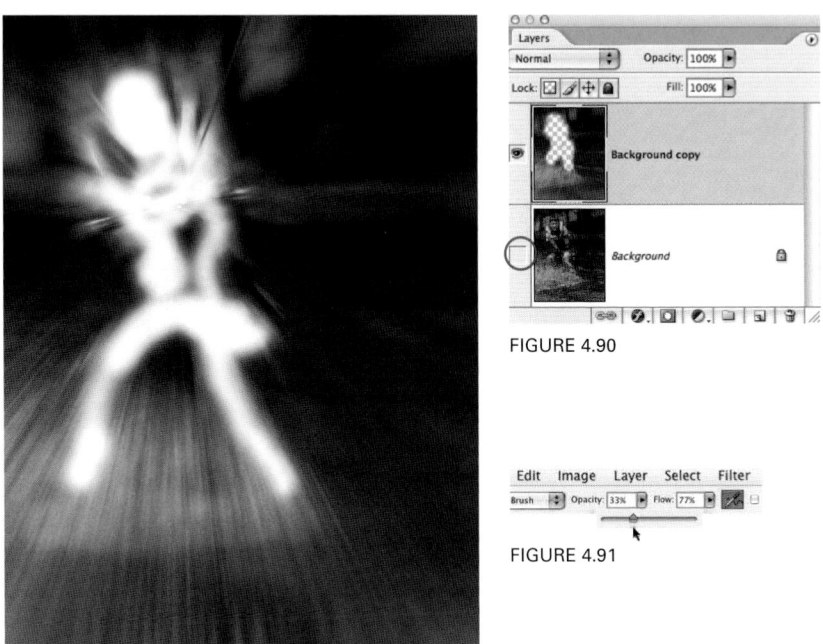

FIGURE 4.90

FIGURE 4.91

FIGURE 4.89

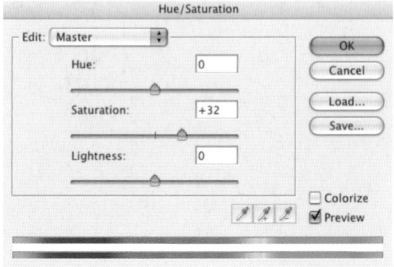

FIGURE 4.92

Next, I used another traditional enhancement: I increased the Saturation (Image > Adjustments > Hue/Saturation) (**Figure 4.92**).

Here's the result (**Figure 4.93**). Compare this image to the opening image in this lesson—that's a big difference.

Continuing on my creative explorations for this image, I imagined a sunburst behind the subject. I use the Lens Flare filter (Filter > Render > Lens Flare) to create the effect of the sun shining through the trees in the background.

With the Lens Flare dialog box open, I positioned the point of light by clicking it and then dragging it around the frame (**Figure 4.94**).

Finally! Here's the result of all that working and playing in Photoshop (**Figure 4.95**).

Hey, I know it's not nice to fool Mother Nature—in this case, placing the sun behind a front-lit subject. If I were submitting a picture for publication to the North American Nature Photography Association (www.nanpa.org), where honesty and integrity are important, I wouldn't do that. But I'm just having fun here.

FIGURE 4.93

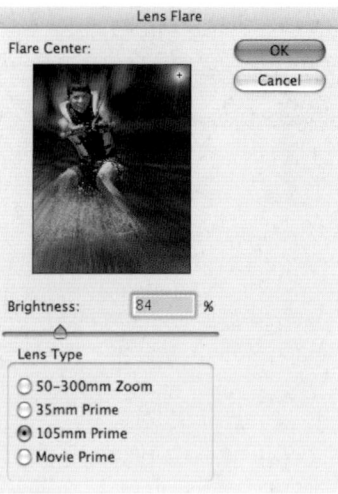

FIGURE 4.94

FIGURE 4.95

▲ FIGURE 4.96

Tech info: Canon EOS
1Ds Mark II, 50mm Macro
lens. Exposure: 1/60 sec. @
f/16. ISO 200.

Earn Your Photoshop Wings

Let's move on to adding just a touch of action to an image,
this time using one of my butterfly photographs (**Figure 4.96**).
My goal was to create the effect that the butterfly was just
beginning to move its wings to take off.

As I did previously, I first created a duplicate layer. To it I
applied the Radial Blur filter. In the Radial Blur dialog box, I
selected Spin as the Blur Method. I played around with the
Amount value to see which degree of the spinning effect I
liked (**Figure 4.97**).

As before, I selected the Eraser tool; then I erased the blur
effect over most of the image. I left just a touch of blur on the leading edge
of the butterfly's wings. Again, it's a good idea to turn off the bottom layer
by clicking the eye icon to check on your erasing skills (**Figure 4.98**).

The blur is very subtle, but that was my goal in this case (**Figure 4.99**). In
the next example, I'll be a little more extreme.

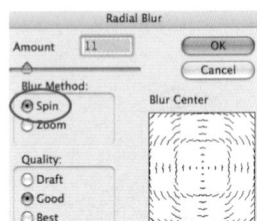

FIGURE 4.97

FIGURE 4.98

FIGURE 4.99

Saddle Up for More Action

To freeze the action in this photograph, I used a shutter speed of 1/500 of a second (**Figure 4.100**). I like the picture, but I wanted to see how intensifying the action would affect the image's impact.

Once again, I applied a Blur filter to a duplicate layer, but this time I selected Motion Blur instead of Radial Blur.

In the Motion Blur dialog box, I set the Angle to 0° because that was the angle at which the horse and rider were moving in my picture. I set the Distance to 198 pixels to create a dramatic effect (**Figure 4.101**). Then I carefully erased the area on the top layer where I didn't want any blur. Because the horse and rider were moving left to right in the frame, I erased the blur in the background and foreground and on most of the horse and rider's body, leaving only a speed trail behind them. Here's the final result (**Figure 4.102**).

Now it's your turn to have some fun. Get moving!

▲ FIGURE 4.100

Tech info: Canon EOS 1D Mark II, 100-400mm IS lens @ 400mm. Exposure: 1/500 sec. @ f/8. ISO 400.

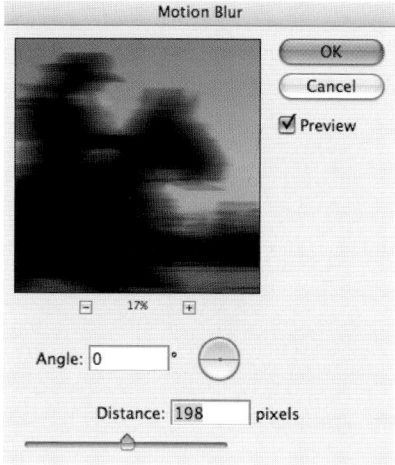

FIGURE 4.101

FIGURE 4.102

Saving the Lion King

Let me begin this lesson by telling you that I'm a proud member of the North American Nature Photography Association (www.nanpa.org). All my fellow members and I stress honesty in photography and digital imaging. If one of our pictures is digitally enhanced or manipulated, we say so: no ifs, ands, or buts. For us, honesty is the best policy.

I'm sharing this photo philosophy with you for three reasons. First, this lesson features a digitally manipulated image, which I'm using to illustrate how you may be able to save one of your own photographs from your computer's outtake folder. Second, I want to stress that if you manipulate an image, it's important to say so, especially if your picture is published. Third, I want you to understand the power of the digital darkroom.

Let's explore that power.

I photographed these lions in courtship while on a safari in Botswana (**Figure 4.103**). It was late in the day, and the sky was overcast, so the straight-out-of-the-camera picture looked a bit flat and soft. That was easy to correct with Levels, Curves, Hue/Saturation, and Brightness/Contrast adjustments.

The big problem with the photo was that the male lion's front left leg (on your right) was cut out of the frame. Photoshop surgery was needed!

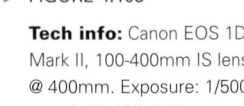

▶ FIGURE 4.103

Tech info: Canon EOS 1D Mark II, 100-400mm IS lens @ 400mm. Exposure: 1/500 sec. @ f/8. ISO 400.

The first step was to increase the canvas size (Image > Canvas Size). In these two screenshots, you can see that I increased the Width of the canvas by one inch on the right side of the image (**Figures 4.104** and **4.105**).

My new document looked like this after I increased the Canvas size (**Figure 4.106**).

Next, I used the Clone Stamp tool to copy existing grass areas into the blank areas of the canvas. Then, I used the Lasso tool to trace (select) part of the lion's right leg (on your left). After making my selection, I copied it and pasted it over the lion's left leg. Doing so placed the copied right leg on a new layer on top of the original document. I used the Move tool, Eraser tool, and Burn and Dodge tools to blend the new leg with the old (**Figure 4.107**).

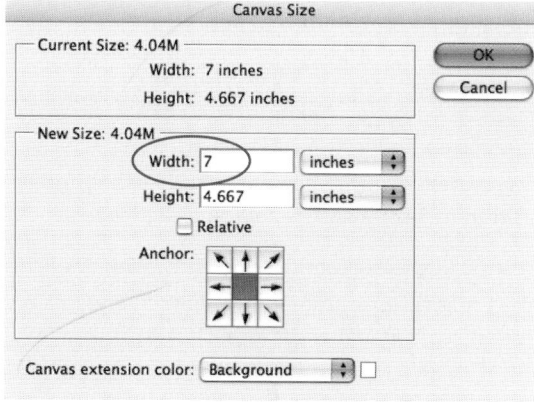

FIGURE 4.104

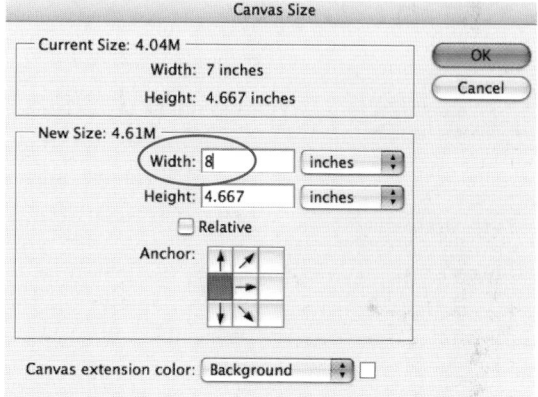

FIGURE 4.105

FIGURE 4.106

FIGURE 4.107

After completing the Photoshop surgery, I decided to enhance my picture's color and contrast. I did that using Levels and by increasing the Saturation. I decided there was too much dead space around the lions, so I used the Crop tool for a tighter crop, which resulted in a more dramatic image.

Now you can see the near-final result of my enhancements (**Figure 4.108**). The new leg was still a bit darker than I wanted it; a bit more work had to be done. What's more, if you look closely, you'll see that the male lion had two right paws!

To hide the flaws in my changes and the fact that the lion now had two right paws, I used a digital photo frame in onOne Software's PhotoFrame Pro 3.0 (**Figure 4.109**).

All you keen-eyed readers probably noticed something else: The background is more out of focus than in the original picture. I blurred the background by making a duplicate layer, blurring the entire layer, and then erasing the areas on the same plane as the lions. That's similar to the effect I would have gotten had I used a longer telephoto lens with less depth of field.

I hope this lesson has given you some ideas about how you can fix your photographs. In the process of fixing and getting published, please remember that honesty is the best policy. The image is your work, but any post-capture enhancement should be duly noted.

So, you may be asking, "How close was Rick to those lions?" Well, they were only about 30 yards away when I took the picture. The moment after I took the picture, they both looked at me (shooting from a safari vehicle) and then slowly walked toward us! When they got to within just a few feet of the vehicle, rather than having lunch, they simply lay down and took a rest. Whew! That was close!

FIGURE 4.108

FIGURE 4.109

Create an Artistic Montage

I always like a challenge, especially when it comes to working and playing in Photoshop. If you like challenges, I think you'll like this lesson. Better yet, take the challenge yourself and try to create your own montage. (These work images, along with all the other work images in this book, are available at www.ricksammon.com.)

FIGURE 4.110

Here was the challenge (from *Popular Photography*): I had to come up with a creative montage using a picture of a car, a picture of a lion, and a picture of a city at nighttime (**Figures 4.110**, **4.111**, and **4.112**). (By the way, I didn't take these photographs.) Note that these pictures weren't the highest-resolution images on the planet; however, they were fine for the challenge and this lesson. The car and lion photographs were the same resolution and height in pixels. The main idea was to combine the

FIGURE 4.111

FIGURE 4.112

images to convey the power of the car. I put on my Photoshop thinking cap and got to work.

Adding motion was my main goal, but that had to wait. First, I had to create the basic montage—the fine-tuning would come later. My progress is documented in this section. (Please keep in mind that there are tons of ways to create a montage in Photoshop; this is just one representation.)

To convey the power of the engine, I decided to show the lion leaping out of the car's grill. I first flipped the image left to right (Image > Rotate Canvas > Flip Canvas Horizontal), because in the original image, the lion was jumping in the wrong direction. Then, I used the Magic Wand tool, and after clicking the Add to Selection icon in the Menu tab to select most of the background (**Figure 4.113**), I cut out that area of the picture by choosing Edit > Cut (**Figure 4.114**).

Because I wanted the lion to appear smaller in the car image, I reduced the size of the lion file by half by going to Image > Image Size and changing the height to 5 inches. I also selected Bicubic Sharper, because famed Photoshop expert Scott Kelby told me that when reducing the size of an image, that's the best technique to use to maximize image quality (**Figure 4.115**).

FIGURE 4.113

FIGURE 4.114

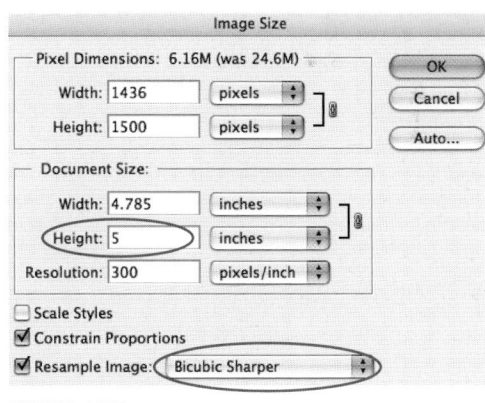

FIGURE 4.115

FIGURE 4.116

With the lion and car files both open, I selected the Move tool, clicked in the lion image, and then dragged that image into the car image (**Figure 4.116**).

My lion cutout wasn't perfect, but that was no problem. I next used the Eraser tool with the Opacity set to 50% in the Options Bar so as not to erase too much too fast; I moved the Eraser around the outline of the lion's body until there was a smooth, unnoticeable transition between the car layer and the lion layer. Then, I used the Blur tool around the edges of the lion's body to soften the border between the lion and the car even more.

You probably noticed that you can see through the lion in this image. That's because I reduced the Opacity of the lion layer (top layer) so I could accurately position the lion.

FIGURE 4.117

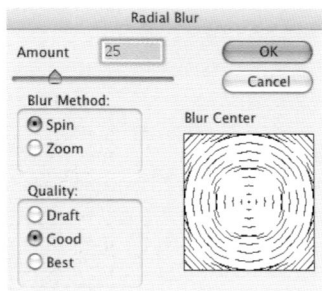

FIGURE 4.118

The lion wasn't in exactly the right position. Plus, I wanted to stretch the lion to give it a greater sense of speed. To do so, with the top layer (the lion image) active, I went to Edit > Transform > Scale. Next, I clicked the lower-left handle (it doesn't matter which handle you choose) and, by moving the handle inward and upward, resized the lion. After clicking inside the Transform box, I positioned the king of beasts over the grill of the car (**Figure 4.117**). I clicked Return to apply the transformation.

At this point, I could clearly see the lion, and I reset the Opacity of the top layer to 100%. Here's the result of my efforts so far (**Figure 4.118**). Later, I would reduce the Opacity of the lion layer for a more subtle view of the animal. I'd also reposition it, again by the using the Transform tool and by clicking inside the Transform box.

The car was parked when the picture was taken, but the power of Photoshop let me easily create the impression that it was moving. Using the Elliptical Marquee tool, I selected the front chrome wheel hub. Then I used the Radial Blur filter and set the wheel spinning (**Figure 4.119**). Then I did the same thing to the back wheel. (I made a mistake here that I'll address at the end of this lesson. I could fix it now, but I want you to guess what it is.)

FIGURE 4.119

FIGURE 4.120

Check this out (**Figure 4.120**). The car is almost on the move. But I need to do more work to set it in motion.

To add motion to the entire car, I decided to use the Motion Blur filter. Using this filter to add a sense of motion and speed to a stationary object requires a two-step process. First, I made a duplicate layer. Then, I applied the degree of blur I wanted in the Motion Blur control panel (**Figure 4.121**).

Now I was getting there (**Figure 4.122**). But something is wrong with this picture. As you keen-eyed photographers and Photoshop users no doubt noticed, there is no driver behind the wheel of the "moving" car! I'll solve that problem in a few moments.

It was time to add the city scene to my picture. In hindsight, I should have started with the city as the background layer; but I didn't have that idea until this point in the process. To add the city, I opened both documents on my screen and then dragged the city picture over the car picture. The city picture appears here as the top layer (**Figure 4.123**). (As you can see, I already flattened the car and lion layers.)

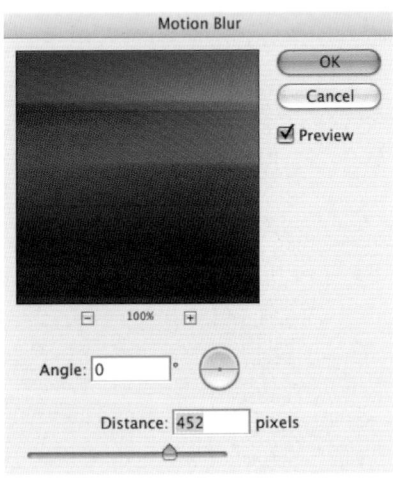

FIGURE 4.121

Guess what? I could still make it the background layer where it belonged. In the Layers palette, after renaming the locked Background layer (by double-clicking on it and then clicking OK in the pop-up dialog box), I clicked the top layer (the city, at this point) and moved it under the car layer. Now the city layer was in the background (**Figures 4.124** and **4.125**). Using the earlier technique of reducing the opacity of the car layer, it was easy to erase the part of the city scene that covered the car.

Here's what I thought was my final montage (**Figure 4.126**). But as I mentioned earlier, the driver was missing. Plus, I felt that I could do more to the image.

FIGURE 4.122

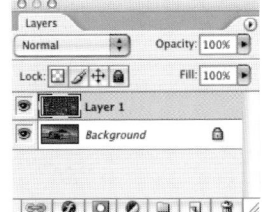

FIGURE 4.123

FIGURE 4.124

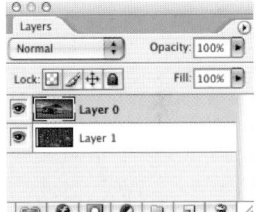

FIGURE 4.125

FIGURE 4.126

For a more dramatic image, I used the Lens Flare filter (Filter > Render > Lens Flare) to add a sunburst to the sky. You can position the flare point anywhere in the scene. The planet in the upper-right corner of the scene came from Flaming Pear's LunaCell Photoshop-compatible plug-in (www. flamingpear.com). I moved the planet into the scene using the same technique I used to add the lion layer. I also painted blurred red and yellow flames on the car by using a brush after selecting red and yellow as my foreground colors in the Foreground/Background Colors at the bottom of the Tool Bar (**Figure 4.127**).

Now it was time to turn on two of the car's front road lights. That was easy: I used the Lens Flare filter again (**Figure 4.128**).

Here's the "no driver" fix. From one of my landscape pictures, I copied part of the sky (**Figure 4.129**). I pasted it into my image and used the Transform feature to move it into position. To fit the sky neatly into the

FIGURE 4.127

FIGURE 4.128

windshield area, I used the Eraser tool to erase parts of the sky that were over the body of the car. The replacement sky hid the fact that there was no driver at the wheel (**Figure 4.130**)! Look closely and you'll see the clouds of a sunset "reflected" on the side of the car. Those come from one of my stock sunset photographs. Again, using the copy and paste and erase technique mentioned earlier, I added them to my montage.

FIGURE 4.129

"How long did it take to create the montage?" you may ask. The process took several hours over a weekend. I was having so much fun and learning so much that I kept working on, and playing with, the image.

What was the mistake I mentioned earlier? Well, the rubber on the tires isn't spinning like the chrome hubs. To fix that, as you can see in the end-result image, I selected the Blur tool and moved it around the tires in a circular motion.

I didn't have to tell you that I missed the stationary tire and no-driver problems during the creation of my initial montage. But I point out my mistakes for a good reason: You'll probably miss stuff and make mistakes while working on images in Photoshop. Don't beat up on yourself. We all make mistakes—and learn from them.

FIGURE 4.130

▲ FIGURE 4.131

Tech info: Canon EOS 1Ds Mark II, 17-40mm lens @ 20mm. Exposure: 1/125 sec. @ f/8. ISO 800.

The Evolution of an Image

When I teach a photography workshop, I stress the importance of visualizing how a picture can be enhanced in the digital darkroom. In doing so, the workshop participants can compose and expose their shots with the digitally enhanced image in mind. At the same time, I also stress the importance of getting the best possible and most creative in-camera image, and not relying on digital darkroom effects to save the day.

To begin this lesson, I'd like to share two pictures I took during a recent workshop that illustrate my second point (**Figures 4.131** and **4.132**). The straight-on picture of the little cowboy is nice, but it's not too creative. That's the shot most of the workshop participants were taking. For a more creative shot, I suggested moving in or zooming the lens tighter and photographing from a different angle. I followed my own advice and got this second shot. I know the picture is dark—I underexposed it so as not to blow out the highlights on the subject's hat.

▲ FIGURE 4.132

Tech info: Canon EOS 1Ds Mark II, 17-40mm lens @ 20mm. Exposure: 1/125 sec. @ f/8. ISO 800.

FIGURE 4.133

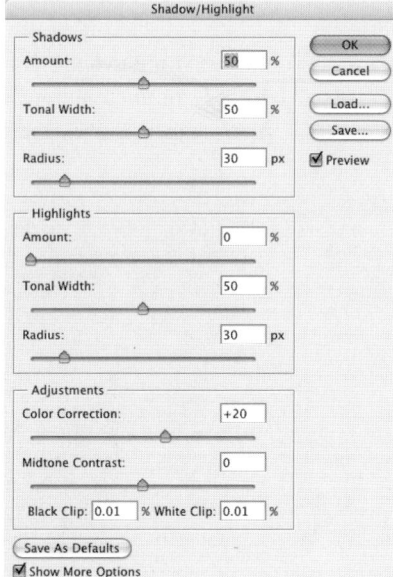

FIGURE 4.134

Here's how the picture would have looked had I exposed for the boy's face (Figure 4.133). As you can see, some of the highlights on the cowboy hat are blown out. (By the way, the chant in my seminar was, "Expose for the highlights!" which is a popular saying (mine!) in all my workshops.)

One of the coolest features in Photoshop is the Shadow/Highlight controls palette (Figure 4.134). By adjusting the sliders, you can control the density of shadows and highlights, making them darker and lighter. Magically, after just a few taps of the stylus on my Wacom tablet, the shadows and highlights were adjusted (Figure 4.135).

When I took the picture, I envisioned a softer look. Photoshop provides dozens of ways to soften a picture (when you include all the Photoshop-compatible plug-ins you can use). For this image, I used a Pastel filter from Nik Software's Color Efex Pro 2.0 (Figure 4.136).

That's the soft touch I wanted; I fine-tuned it to my personal preference by using the sliders in the Pastel filter's interface. However, the picture was a bit too light (Figure 4.137).

FIGURE 4.135

FIGURE 4.136

FIGURE 4.137

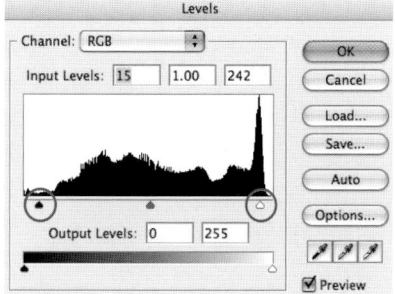

FIGURE 4.138

FIGURE 4.139

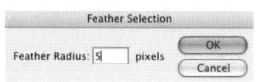

FIGURE 4.140

While working in a Levels Adjustment Layer, I moved the shadow slider on the left to just inside the mountain range in the histogram to darken the image. After doing so, I was not 100 percent pleased with the brightness of the image, so I moved the highlight slider on the right to just inside the mountain range (Figure 4.138). To give the image an extra-soft touch, I decided to apply the Vignette (selection) Action (which resides in the Frames group of Actions). But first, I had a job to do.

I made my selection with the Rectangular Marquee in the Tool Bar by clicking inside the image and making a selection about ½ inch into the frame. My selection is indicated by "marching ants" around the inside of the frame (Figure 4.139).

If you ever—and I mean ever—make a selection, don't skip this step! You need to choose a Feather Radius (Select > Feather). Here's why: The number you select affects the softness (or hardness) of the vignetting. For this image, I selected a Feather Radius of 5 (Figure 4.140).

Here's the result of using a Feather Radius of 5, but it wasn't exactly what wanted (Figure 4.141).

I tried a Feather Radius of 75 for a more gradual vignetting effect. Now my picture had the soft touch I was looking for (Figure 4.142).

FIGURE 4.141

FIGURE 4.142

FIGURE 4.143

This lesson is entitled "The Evolution of an Image" for a good reason: to illustrate my point that there are endless possibilities for your pictures in the digital darkroom. To soften the image even further, I subdued the colors using a Hue/Saturation Adjustment Layer. You may want to try that on some of your scanned super-saturated pictures taken with highly saturated Kodak or Fuji films. You may be surprised and pleased with a subtler image.

Here's the result of removing a fair amount of color from the image (Figure 4.143).

The Never-Ending Quest

Working and playing in Photoshop CS2 is a never-ending quest; if you use your imagination and experiment with Photoshop's different tools and features, you can keep coming up with new and different versions of a photograph in the never-ending search for a creative image. This lesson and the following one offer a few examples of that never-ending quest. Some of these techniques have been mentioned earlier in this book, but I thought you might like to see how they look when applied to another image.

Let's begin with a picture I took of two horses running on the Ponderosa Ranch in Seneca, Oregon (**Figure 4.144**).

As you read in "Black-and-White and Beyond," a good way to get a black-and-white image is to use Channel Mixer (Image > Adjustments > Channel Mixer > check Monochrome) rather than creating a grayscale image (Image > Mode > Grayscale) (**Figures 4.145** and **4.146**).

Here you can see how I used the Sepia Toning (layer) Action (from the Image Effects group of Actions) to create a nice sepia-toned image effortlessly (**Figure 4.147**).

And look what happened to my straight shot when I applied the Angled Strokes filter (Filter > Brush Strokes > Angled Strokes) (**Figures 4.148** and **4.149**).

▶ FIGURE 4.144

Tech info: Canon EOS 1D Mark II, 100-400mm IS lens @ 400mm. Exposure: 1/500 sec. @ f/8. ISO 400.

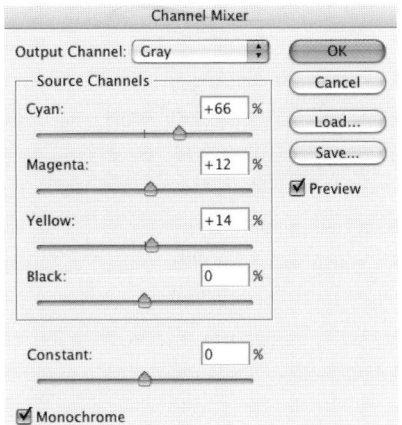

FIGURE 4.145

FIGURE 4.146

FIGURE 4.147

Angled Strokes (33.3%)

▶ 🗀 Artistic
▼ 🗀 Brush Strokes

Accented Edges | Angled Strokes | Crosshatch

Dark Strokes | Ink Outlines | Spatter

Sprayed Strokes | Sumi-e

▶ 🗀 Distort
▶ 🗀 Sketch
▶ 🗀 Stylize
▶ 🗀 Texture

OK
Default

Angled Strokes

Direction Balance   17
Stroke Length   26
Sharpness   4

Angled Strokes

33.3%

FIGURE 4.148

FIGURE 4.149

Want to create a frame that no one else on the planet has ever created? Here's how I did this one (**Figure 4.150**).

I clicked the Eraser tool in the Tool Bar and then selected an artistic brush from the Brush Preset picker by clicking the Brush drop-down menu in the Menu Bar. (If you don't see a brush you like, you can load additional brushes by clicking the fly-out arrow at the top-right of the Brush Preset picker.) Then, I moved the Eraser tool around the edge of my image to erase to the background color (which I selected at the bottom of the Tool Bar)—white, in this example.

FIGURE 4.150

FIGURE 4.151

Here's the effect of using black as the background color (**Figure 4.151**).

You can also combine more than one creative effect for a unique and original picture. Here, I used two plug-ins, the Midnight Sepia filter in Nik Software's Color Efex Pro 2.0 (**Figure 4.152**) and the Camera frame in onOne Software's PhotoFrame 3.0 (**Figure 4.153**), to create a unique image (**Figure 4.154**).

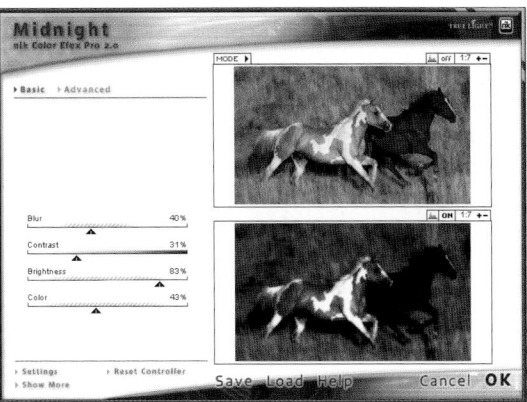

FIGURE 4.152

FIGURE 4.153

FIGURE 4.154

Speaking of frames, you can use the Vignette (selection) Action (from the Frames group of Actions) to add an artistic frame to a picture. Here, I used a Feather Radius of 5, which produced a pronounced variation between the image and the background color, which was set to white (Figure 4.155).

I got a soft vignette effect by selecting a larger feather radius (50, in this example) (Figure 4.156).

I could go on and on and on with this image, but that's it for now. Check out the next section, "Variations on a Theme," to see how you can use other creative effects to create a more artistic image. It's all part of the quest.

FIGURE 4.155

FIGURE 4.156

▲ FIGURE 4.157

Tech info: Canon EOS
1Ds Mark II, 17-40mm lens
@ 17mm. Exposure: 1/125
sec. @ f/8. ISO 100.

Variations on a Theme

By now you know where to find the adjustments, filters, and other features in Photoshop that help you enhance your pictures with creative and artistic effects. In this lesson I'd just like to show you some variations on a theme, along with instructions on how to get to the individual creative effects.

For this lesson, I'll use a picture I took of the Leslie Hotel in Miami's South Beach (**Figure 4.157**). Let's look at a few of the endless possibilities you can explore in Photoshop. For each of these effects, I went back to the original image and used the default settings for each adjustment or filter, except for Neon Glow, for which I had the color yellow selected.

◆ Invert (Image > Adjustments > Invert). The colors are inverted, as you'd see in a film negative (**Figure 4.158**).

- Invert with Fade (Image > Adjustments > Invert, and then Edit > Fade Invert and in the Fade dialog box that appears select the Difference mode). As always, fading a filter or effect can result in unusual, unique, and sometimes unexpected results (**Figure 4.159**).

- Posterize 3 (Image > Adjustments > Posterize, and in the Posterize dialog box that appears, enter 3 in the Levels field) (**Figure 4.160**). Pop artist Peter Max created images with a similar posterized effect.

- Posterize 4 (Image > Adjustments > Posterize, and in the Posterize dialog box that appears, enter 4 in the Levels field) (**Figure 4.161**). This is another Peter Max–type posterized image.

FIGURE 4.158

FIGURE 4.159

FIGURE 4.160

FIGURE 4.161

- Poster Edges (Filter > Artistic > Poster Edges). This image is sort of cartoonish, but it's fun nonetheless (**Figure 4.162**).

- Glowing Edges (Filter > Stylize > Glowing Edges). Objects appear to be outlined with neon lights (**Figure 4.163**).

- Neon Glow (Filter > Artistic > Neon Glow, with Yellow selected) (**Figure 4.164**). Remember to experiment with different colors for different effects.

- Craquelure (Filter > Texture > Craquelure). This option adds a creative texture to an image (**Figure 4.165**).

- Hue set to –86 (Image > Adjustments > Hue/Saturation, and in the Hue/Saturation dialog box that appears, set Hue to –86) (**Figure 4.166**). You can change all the colors in a scene by changing the hue.

- Hue set to +86 (Image > Adjustments > Hue/Saturation, and in the Hue/Saturation dialog box that appears, set Hue to +86) (**Figure 4.167**). Color-change possibilities are endless with hue adjustments.

I end the lessons with the same inspiration I used to lead off this book: the idea of dreaming. Again, pleasant Photoshop dreams.

FIGURE 4.162

FIGURE 4.163

FIGURE 4.164

FIGURE 4.165

FIGURE 4.166

FIGURE 4.167

5 The Photographic Image

I BEGAN THIS BOOK with a discussion about the photographic idea—seeing creatively and visualizing the end result. Chapter 1, "The Photographic Idea," is one of the most important chapters in this book, because if you don't have an idea of what you want to record with your camera, then you're clueless about the story the photograph should tell or the emotion it creates for the viewer.

Sure, you can take fun shots and play around with them in Photoshop to your heart's content. I do it all the time. It's OK to have fun! But I take my photography very seriously. I consider myself a photographer first and foremost, striving to get the best possible in-camera image. Therefore, I thought a logical final chapter for this book would be about the *image*—how I get my images—what I'm thinking and feeling when I look through my camera's viewfinder.

To illustrate this chapter, I'll share with you some photographs I took on a 2006 trip to "The Land of the Thunder Dragon," more commonly known as Bhutan, a remote Himalayan Kingdom that sits on the right shoulder of India.

LET'S ENCOUNTER THE DRAGON.

See the Story

Bhutan is perhaps the most magical place that my wife, Susan, and I have visited, and I say that having been to nearly 100 countries in my travels around the planet. But even in such a magical place, great images don't just happen. You can't wave a magic wand or chant an incantation to get a great shot. You need to understand your subject matter, know the story you want to tell, and be prepared to get involved.

Environmental Portraits

▼ FIGURE 5.1

Tech info: Canon EOS 1Ds Mark II, Canon 17-40mm lens @ 17mm. Exposure: 1/125 sec. @ f/11. ISO 200.

I took this picture, and the opening picture for this chapter, at the Dzong-drakha festival, a sacred annual celebration that has remained basically unchanged for centuries (**Figure 5.1**). Knowing the importance and reverence of the festival to the local residents, I was especially careful not to

intrude on the performance, keeping my shooting position on the perimeter of the blessed ground.

The image on the opposite page is what I call an *environmental portrait*: a subject pictured in its environment. My goal was to capture the Black Hat dancer's beautiful outfit, as well as the wondrous and magical feeling of the festival.

Using my wide-angle zoom lens set at the widest setting, I selected a small f-stop (f/11) and, using the focus lock on my camera, set the focus one-third into the scene (as opposed to letting the camera focus on the subject). Once the focus point was set, while still holding down the shutter-release button, I recomposed the photograph and took the picture. Had I let the camera focus on the subject, the background would have been softer (a bit out of focus). When you want as much of the scene in focus as possible, try this technique. It's especially useful in landscape photography, when you want everything from the foreground to the distant background in focus.

▲ FIGURE 5.2

Tech info: Canon EOS 1D Mark II, Canon 70-200mm IS lens @ 200mm. Exposure: 1/125 sec. @ f/4.5. ISO 400.

Know the Subject

Check out the photograph above. Because the subject's eyes are closed, you may think that I missed this shot (**Figure 5.2**). Actually, the dancer is in a trance-like state, and this picture captures that moment—the moment I wanted to capture.

To isolate the subject from the background, I used my telephoto zoom lens set at a wide aperture, so that when I focused on the subject, the background was out of focus. As a result, your attention is focused on the dancer and his entranced expression.

Capture the Peak of Action

The lure of festivals brought me to Bhutan, and the annual Paro festival was the main draw. These Lords of the Cremation Ground dancers at that festival burst onto the scene at top speed (Figure 5.3). I used a fast shutter speed to stop the action. I also set my camera on rapid frame advance so that I caught the dancers in mid-step with their feet off the ground. This conveyed the feeling of movement and the sense that the action was at its high point. When the subject is moving, think in terms of capturing the peak of action.

▼ FIGURE 5.3

Tech info: Canon EOS 1D Mark II, Canon 70-200mm IS lens @ 200mm. Exposure: 1/250 sec. @ f/8. ISO 400.

Posed Portraits

"I guess Rick has the personality to just walk up to people and take their picture." That's what a student said to one of my workshop groups recently, and it's probably true. However, the personality I project—my feeling and emotion—helps me capture subjects the way I envision them. Different subjects require different approaches: happy, serious, enthusiastic, and so on. I'm well aware of the need to be sensitive to different personalities in different situations.

For this picture of a young girl in a remote village, I approached her with an attitude of respect and a feeling of warmth (**Figure 5.4**). I asked her if I could take her picture beforehand, and then I showed her the results of the photo session on the LCD screen on the back of my camera. I worked fast, taking only a few shots so I didn't overstay my welcome.

"Why is he taking my picture?" the young girl asked my guide. Through him, I explained, "Because as I walked down the street of your village, filled with dozens of people, your beautiful face caught my eye." To me, she had the most striking face in the village. It's usually someone's face that attracts me to a subject. When I first saw the girl, she was standing in the harsh sunlight. For a more flattering picture, one with soft and even light, I asked her to move into the shade. She wrapped her arm around the pole. What a perfect model!

Looking at the girl's face I feel, as I do with many portraits, a bit melancholy knowing that I'll probably never see this stranger in a strange land again. And the subject may feel this, too! But I have the memory and the picture. The subject only has the memory, which fades in time.

▼ FIGURE 5.4

Tech info: Canon EOS 1D Mark II, Canon 70-200mm IS lens @ 100mm. Exposure: 1/125 sec. @ f/5.6. ISO 400.

▲ FIGURE 5.5

Tech info: Canon
EOS 1Ds Mark II, Canon
17-40mm lens @ 20mm.
Exposure: 1/125 sec. @ f/8.
ISO 400.

Compose Carefully

This picture of a young monk with a *dzong* (fortress and temple) in the background is one of my favorites from the trip (**Figure 5.5**). I photographed dozens of monks and many *dzongs*, but here I wanted to show both subjects, isolating each of them. After asking the monk if I could take his picture, I composed the scene with him way off center and then framed the shot so that I didn't cut off any of the *dzong*.

As you can tell, the image is cropped to the panoramic format. I feel that cropping made the picture look more interesting than a full-frame shot.

As with earlier pictures in this chapter, I used a wide-angle setting on my zoom lens, used a small f-stop, and focused one-third into the scene. As a result, the entire scene was in focus.

Don't Settle for Less

▶ FIGURE 5.6

Tech info: Canon EOS
1Ds Mark II, Canon
17-40mm lens @ 20mm.
Exposure: 1/125 sec. @ f/8.
ISO 400.

On my first day in Thimphu, Bhutan's capital city, I took several photographs of this man smoking a pipe while sitting by some prayer wheels at the Memorial Chorten (religious structure). This is not one of them (**Figure 5.6**). Those pictures were OK, but the light level was low and flat, and I felt I could do better. I knew that I could go back the next day, so I warmed up by taking pictures and getting him used to having me around.

This picture is my favorite from my second photo session. One reason is that you can see the smoke.

The message of this little homily is, "Don't settle for second best." Go for the best possible photograph you can take.

Be Patient

Most of the time, I walk up to a subject and ask, "May I take your picture?" Sometimes, however, I stand in one position and wait for the subject to walk into the frame, as I did for this photograph of a woman at some of the prayer wheels at the Memorial Chorten (**Figure 5.7**). As with the picture of the young girl, the woman's face attracted me to her.

I stood there for maybe 10 minutes as she walked around and around the prayer wheels, smiling at her as she walked by. On one pass, I raised my camera and began the photo session. To capture her movement, I set my camera on rapid frame advance. This is one of 10 frames from that sequence.

▼ FIGURE 5.7

Tech info: Canon EOS 1Ds Mark II, Canon 17-40mm lens @ 20mm. Exposure: 1/125 sec. @ f/8. ISO 400.

▲ FIGURE 5.8

Tech info: Canon EOS
1Ds Mark II, Canon
17-40mm lens @ 20mm.
Exposure: 1/250 sec. @ f/8.
ISO 800.

Be Prepared

Perhaps one of the most important aspects of photography is being prepared for the unexpected. That means having your camera set to capture a fleeting subject or subjects, such as these young monks dashing out of a temple to have their lunch (**Figure 5.8**).

Usually, I walk around with two digital SLRs hanging from my shoulders: one with a telephoto zoom and one with a wide-angle zoom. The two lenses help me capture different views quickly and easily.

Both cameras are set on Program (the mode that enables the camera to automatically set the f-stop and aperture for the correct exposure) so I can point and shoot and at least get a nice shot. Then, I may switch to Aperture Priority (when depth of field is important) or Shutter Priority (when motion is important) to fine-tune the image. All digital SLRs feature these exposure modes.

Be There

While driving through the Punakha valley, we spotted a school and asked our guide, Chencho, if we could visit. I enjoy photographing kids tremendously, so I knew this would be a good photo session.

I guess I do have the personality to walk up to people and take their picture. Here, I calmly entered the schoolyard during the school's morning prayer and song, and clicked away (**Figure 5.9**). I became part of the scene—being in just the right place at just the right time.

The lighting conditions were ideal. The overcast sky provided a soft light on the faces of all the subjects, so they were evenly illuminated. If you plan to photograph a person outdoors, pray for soft light.

▼ FIGURE 5.9

Tech info: Canon EOS 1Ds Mark II, Canon 17-40mm lens @ 17mm. Exposure: 1/250 sec. @ f/8. ISO 400.

See Beyond the Frame

It's not only what you see in the viewfinder that makes a good photographic image. Often, you need to see beyond the single frame and look for the larger story; you need to perceive how the subject fits into the overall environment. Sometimes a story is better told in more than one image, or from a unique perspective that captures what you as the photographer experienced, whether trekking up a mountain path or viewing a scene through fluttering prayer flags.

Think Slide Show

Sometimes, it takes more than a single image to tell a story—especially when you want to put together a slide show, Web gallery, or PDF presentation. In those situations, and with those thoughts in mind, it's good to take a set or series of pictures.

To tell the story of archery in Bhutan, the national sport played throughout the kingdom, I took many pictures. These are two of my favorites: a close-up of an archer dressed in a *gho* (traditional dress), and a picture of an archer standing (unbelievably) right next to a target (**Figures 5.10** and **5.11**). The *really* unbelievable part is that the archers walk into position, aim, and shoot in a matter of seconds—and hit the far-off target more often than you might imagine—without hitting any of the other archers!

▲ FIGURE 5.10

Tech info: Canon EOS 1D Mark II, Canon 70-200mm IS lens @ 200mm. Exposure: 1/125 sec. @ f/2.8. ISO 400.

Create a Sense of Depth

You see the world in three dimensions: height, width, and depth. Cameras see only two: height and width. One way to create a sense of depth is to include a foreground subject. On the next page, I framed the *stupas* (religious structures) at Dochu La mountain pass with hundreds of prayer flags (**Figure 5.12**).

By using a wide-angle zoom lens and a small f-stop setting on the lens, and by focusing one-third into the scene, I was able to capture all the elements in the frame in sharp focus—just the way I saw it with my eyes.

◀ FIGURE 5.11

Tech info: Canon EOS 1D Mark II, Canon 70-200mm IS lens @ 200mm. Exposure: 1/125 sec. @ f/4.5. ISO 400.

▼ FIGURE 5.12

Tech info: Canon EOS 1Ds Mark II, Canon 17-40mm lens @ 17mm. Exposure: 1/125 sec. @ f/11. ISO 400.

▲ FIGURE 5.13

Tech info: Canon EOS 1Ds Mark II, Canon 17-40mm lens @ 17mm. Exposure: 1/60 sec. @ f/8. ISO 100.

Be on the Lookout

If you've ever been to a theme park or other tourist attraction, you've seen photo spots—locations suggested for good pictures. You may be tempted to pass them up, believing them to be artificial or mundane. Don't. When I travel, I ask my guides for spots, often lookouts, where tourists take pictures. I shoot photographs, like this picture of the Punakha Dzong, at these spots to round out my presentations (**Figure 5.13**). Don't overlook these lookouts. You can get some nice shots from them.

Get Lucky!

Many people tell me how lucky I am to travel to places like Bhutan and get pictures like the one of Tiger's Nest Temple on the next page (**Figure 5.14**). Yes, I'm very lucky. But I've found that the harder I work, the luckier I become.

▶ FIGURE 5.14

Tech info: Canon EOS 1D Mark II, Canon 70-200mm IS lens @ 150mm. Exposure: 1/125 sec. @ f/5.6. ISO 400.

Your "luck" for taking a picture like this would include making a hike from about 7,500 to 10,000 feet over a winding, rocky, slippery path. Even though I'm in good shape, this was the hardest hike I've ever been on. And, of course, the luck that took me to Bhutan came after years of hard work.

Have Fun!

Ask yourself this question: "What does my photography mean to me?" Now close your eyes and think carefully about your answer for a few minutes, and then come back.

I do that exercise at my workshops. It's interesting, because there are so many different answers.

For me, photography is fun, plain and simple. I do work hard, but it's work I really enjoy. The reward of getting a good shot—a keeper—is tremendous. In this picture, I'm having a blast (**Figure 5.15**), showing the monks one of my magic tricks. In doing so, I showed them that I'm honestly interested in them, not just interested in taking their pictures.

There is a great expression: If you love what you do, you never have to work a day in your life. Have fun with your photography, and don't let all the technical aspects of picture-taking get in the way.

Fasten Your Seatbelts

The last photograph in this book is one of the last I took on our Bhutan adventure (**Figure 5.16**). It's not my best image from the trip, but it tells an interesting story.

Landing at the Paro airport, the only airport in Bhutan, is, well…unique. It's one of the most unusual landings in the civilized world. The Royal Druk Airbus has a distinctive challenge: It has to weave its way over and around the mountains, turning left and right and arcing up and down, to make the landing on a runway that ends relatively close to the face of a mountain. It's like a rollercoaster in the air! After one bank, when I looked out the window, I swore the mountain was only 300 feet away from the tip of the wing. Susan and I and our fellow passengers were all laughing at what we saw to cover up our nervousness. We were all happy when the rollercoaster of a ride in the sky ended and the plane finally landed.

And just for the record, the take-off was just as thrilling.

◀ FIGURE 5.15

Tech info: Canon EOS 1Ds
Mark II, Canon 17-40mm
lens @ 17mm. Exposure:
1/125 sec. @ f/11. ISO 400.
Photo: Susan Sammon

▲ FIGURE 5.16

Tech info: Canon EOS 1Ds Mark II, Canon
17-40mm lens @ 40mm. Exposure: 1/125
sec. @ f/11. ISO 200.

Index

cool light, 64
Cooling Filter (80), 22
Copy command, 98, 104
copyright, xiv
cowboy pictures, 2–12, 126–128,
        164–167
Craquelure filter, 176
creative images, 3, 6–7, 31, 114.
        See also artistic techniques
Crop tool, 16, 22, 100, 154
cropping pictures, 16, 22, 100,
        145, 154
Cuban friend pictures, 94–95,
        129–131
Curves command
    adjusting contrast with, 86
    and Adjustment Layers, 56
    and black-and-white images, 126
    and Channel Mixer, 130
    darkening edges with, 41
    darkening images with, 120, 142
    and flat images, 152
    increasing brightness with, 60
    increasing saturation with, 18
    vs. Levels command, 42
    warming up image with, 92

D

Dali, Salvador, 59, 94
Darken mode, 123
darkening-edges technique, 40–41,
        44, 86
darkroom effects, 42, 164. *See also*
        digital darkroom
Density slider, 21, 22, 66
depth of field, 7, 186
desaturating images, 15, 128. *See*
        also Saturation slider
destructive editing, 56
Diffuse Glow filter, 13, 116, 134
diffusers, 10
digital darkroom
    avoiding over-reliance on, 164
    enhancing landscapes in, 42, 44
    power of Photoshop in, 59, 152
    saving time in, 12

digital frames, 22, 154
digital negatives, 24
digital noise, 36, 84
digital photography, 31, 152. *See*
        also photography
digital SLR cameras, 16, 84, 86,
        138, 186
Dodge tool, 36, 147, 153
Drop Shadow frame, 22
Dry Brush filter, 78
Dry Media Brushes, 119
Duotone images, 130–131
Duplex Monochrome effect, 79
dzong picture, 184
Dzongdrakha festival pictures,
        180–181

E

e-cards, 23
edges
    blurring/softening, 34, 158
    darkening, 40–41, 44, 45, 86
    leaving space around, 22
elephant picture, 56
Elliptical Marquee tool, 40, 159
Emulsion Frame, 116
enhancing images. *See* image
        enhancement
environmental portraits, 180–181
Eraser tool
    erasing background with, 88, 91,
        136, 170
    erasing face with, 48
    erasing sky with, 163
    reducing opacity of, 147
    smoothing area between two
        images with, 92
    smoothing transitions with, 150,
        153, 158
erasing
    with Eraser tool. *See* Eraser tool
    with Layer Mask, 35
exposure settings, 4, 26
Eyedropper tool, 140, 145

photography
    creative tools for, 31
    having fun with, 192
    honesty in, 152, 154
    importance of patience in, 185
    preparing for unexpected in, 186
    role of Photoshop in, 31
    workshops, 4, 164, 192
Photography Association, North
    American Nature, 148, 152
Photoshop. *See also* specific
    commands/tools
    Actions, 72–75, 166, 168, 173
    artistic techniques. *See* artistic
        techniques
    Camera Raw. *See* Camera Raw
    as creative tool, 31
    digital frames, 22–23
    enhancing landscapes with,
        42–45
    enhancing portraits with, 46–49
    filters. *See* filters
    opening raw files in, 25
    plug-ins, 70, 76, 79, 116, 162
    setting History States for, 139
    straightening images in, 32
Photoshop Diet technique, 59, 94
picture background. *See*
    background
pictures. *See also* images
    adding borders to, 36
    avoiding dead space in, 7
    backgrounds for, 8–9
    capturing details in, 10
    composing, 6–7, 9, 10, 184
    copyright considerations, xiv
    creating sense of depth in, 188
    cropping, 16, 22, 100, 145, 154
    downloading from author's Web
        site, xiii
    enhancing. *See* image
        enhancement
    "hand painting," 118
    horizontal *vs.* vertical, 8
    mirroring, 98

    posterizing, 108–111, 175
    reducing size of, 157
    rotating, 32, 157
    sharing, 23
    sharpening areas in, 25, 35–36, 54
    solarizing, 111
    speed-aging, 72–73
    stopping/blurring action in, 12
    straightening, 32
    taking *vs.* making, 6
    telling stories with, 10, 179,
        180, 188
    visualizing end result for, 3, 13, 14
Pinhole Camera effect, 84–87
pinhole cameras, 84, 86
plug-ins, 70, 76, 79, 116, 162
Ponderosa Ranch pictures, 4,
    136–137, 168–173
pop art, 111
Popular Photography, 156
portraits, 46–49, 86, 122, 180–181,
    183
posed portraits, 183
Poster Edges filter, 176
posterizing images, 108–111, 175
prayer-flags picture, 188, 189
prayer-wheel picture, 185
professional photographers, 32, 42,
    84. *See also* photographers
Program mode, 186
PSD files, 57
Punakha Dzong picture, 190

Q

Quadtone images, 131
Quark Expeditions, 14

R

Radial Blur filter, 147, 150, 159
rain effect. *See* Light Rain Action
rainy-day pictures, 75
raw files, 24–29
"Raw Rules" chant, 24
Rectangular Marquee tool, 36, 44
reflections, 10, 16, 98–103